In: Laws and Legislation

AF764729

STATE SECRETS PROTECTION ACT

LAWS AND LEGISLATION

State Secrets Protection Act
Lara H. Nellington
2009 ISBN: 978-1-60692-711-3

In: Laws and Legislation

STATE SECRETS PROTECTION ACT

LARA H. NELLINGTON
EDITOR

Nova Science Publishers, Inc.
New York

Copyright © 2009 by Nova Science Publishers, Inc.

All rights reserved. No part of this book may be reproduced, stored in a retrieval system or transmitted in any form or by any means: electronic, electrostatic, magnetic, tape, mechanical photocopying, recording or otherwise without the written permission of the Publisher.

For permission to use material from this book please contact us:
Telephone 631-231-7269; Fax 631-231-8175
Web Site: http://www.novapublishers.com

NOTICE TO THE READER

The Publisher has taken reasonable care in the preparation of this book, but makes no expressed or implied warranty of any kind and assumes no responsibility for any errors or omissions. No liability is assumed for incidental or consequential damages in connection with or arising out of information contained in this book. The Publisher shall not be liable for any special, consequential, or exemplary damages resulting, in whole or in part, from the readers' use of, or reliance upon, this material.

Independent verification should be sought for any data, advice or recommendations contained in this book. In addition, no responsibility is assumed by the publisher for any injury and/or damage to persons or property arising from any methods, products, instructions, ideas or otherwise contained in this publication.

This publication is designed to provide accurate and authoritative information with regard to the subject matter covered herein. It is sold with the clear understanding that the Publisher is not engaged in rendering legal or any other professional services. If legal or any other expert assistance is required, the services of a competent person should be sought. FROM A DECLARATION OF PARTICIPANTS JOINTLY ADOPTED BY A COMMITTEE OF THE AMERICAN BAR ASSOCIATION AND A COMMITTEE OF PUBLISHERS.

LIBRARY OF CONGRESS CATALOGING-IN-PUBLICATION DATA

Available Upon Request

ISBN: 978-1-60692-711-3

Published by Nova Science Publishers, Inc. † New York

CONTENTS

PREFACE

The ''state secrets privilege'' is a common law rule of evidence that the Federal Government can invoke to prevent materials from being publicly disclosed in civil court proceedings, if the Government establishes that such disclosure would harm the Nation. In the early 1970s, Congress considered including a state secrets provision in the Federal Rules of Evidence, but it ultimately decided not to include any privileges. Although numerous laws govern the handling of classified documents and other information that may implicate state secrets in specific contexts, the state secrets privilege has never been codified in statute.

In: State Secrets Protection Act
Editor: Lara H. Nellington
ISBN 978-1-60692-711-3
© 2009 Nova Science Publishers, Inc.

Chapter 1

S. 2533: A BILL IN THE SENATE OF THE UNITED STATES (110TH CONGRESS 2D SESSION)

To enact a safe, fair, and responsible state secrets privilege Act

JANUARY 22 (legislative day, JANUARY 3), 2008
Mr. KENNEDY (for himself, Mr. SPECTER, and Mr. LEAHY) introduced the following bill; which was read twice and referred to the Committee on the Judiciary

Be it enacted by the Senate and House of Representatives of the United States of America in Congress assembled

Section 1. Short Title

This Act may be cited as the "State Secrets Protection Act".

Section 2. State Secrets Protection

(a) IN GENERAL.—Title 28 of the United States Code is amended by adding after chapter 180, the following:

"CHAPTER 181—STATE SECRETS PROTECTION

"§ 4051. Definition

"In this chapter, the term 'state secret' refers to any information that, if disclosed publicly, would be reasonably likely to cause significant harm to the national defense or foreign relations of the United States.

"§ 4052. Rules Governing Procedures Related to this Chapter

"(a) DOCUMENTS.—A Federal court—

"(1) shall determine which filings, motions, and affidavits, or portions thereof, submitted under this chapter shall be submitted ex parte;

"(2) may order a party to provide a redacted, unclassified, or summary substitute of a filing, motion, or affidavit to other parties; and

"(3) shall make decisions under this subsection taking into consideration the interests of justice and national security.

"(b) HEARINGS.—

"(1) IN CAMERA HEARINGS.—

"(A) IN GENERAL.—Except as provided in subparagraph (B), all hearings under this chapter shall be conducted in camera.

"(B) EXCEPTION.—A court may not conduct a hearing under this chapter in camera based on the assertion of the state secrets privilege if the court determines that the hearing relates only to a question of law and does not present a risk of revealing state secrets.

"(2) EX PARTE HEARINGS.—A Federal court may conduct hearings or portions thereof ex parte if the court determines, following in camera review of the evidence, that the interests of justice and national security cannot adequately be protected through the measures described in subsections (c) and (d).

"(3) RECORD OF HEARINGS.—The court shall preserve the record of all hearings conducted under this chapter for use in the event of an appeal. The court shall seal all records to the extent necessary to protect national security.

"(c) ATTORNEY SECURITY CLEARANCES.—

"(1) IN GENERAL.—A Federal court shall, at the request of the United States, limit participation in hearings conducted under this chapter, or access to motions or affidavits submitted under this chapter, to attorneys with appropriate security clearances, if the court determines that limiting participation in that manner would serve the interests of national security. The court may also appoint a guardian ad litem with the necessary security clearances to represent any party for the purposes of any hearing conducted under this chapter.

"(2) STAYS.—During the pendency of an application for security clearance by an attorney representing a party in a hearing conducted under this chapter, the court may suspend proceedings if the court determines that such a suspension would serve the interests of justice.

"(d) PROTECTIVE ORDERS.—A Federal court may issue a protective order governing any information or evidence disclosed or discussed at any hearing conducted under this chapter if the court determines that issuing such an order is necessary to protect national security.

"(e) OPINIONS AND ORDERS.—Any opinions or orders issued under this chapter may be issued under sealor in redacted versions if, and to the extent that, the court determines that such measure is necessary to protect national security.

"(f) SPECIAL MASTERS.—A Federal court may appoint a special master or other independent advisor who holds the necessary security clearances to assist the court in handling a matter subject to this chapter.

" 4053. Procedures for Answering a Complaint

"(a) INTERVENTION.—The United States may intervene in any civil action in order to protect information the Government determines may be subject to the state secrets privilege.

"(b) IMPERMISSIBLE AS GROUNDS FOR DISMISSAL PRIOR TO HEARINGS.—Except as provided in section 4055, the state secrets privilege shall not constitute grounds for dismissal of a case or claim. A ruling on a motion to dismiss, or for summary judgment, based onthe state secrets privilege shall be deferred pending completion of the discovery and pretrial hearings provided under this chapter.

"(c) PLEADING STATE SECRETS.—In answering a complaint, if the United States or an officer or agency of the United States is a party to the litigation, the United States may plead the state secrets privilege in response to any allegation in any individual claim or counterclaim if the admission or denial of that allegation in that individual claim or counterclaim would itself divulge a state secret to another party or the public. If the United States has intervened in a civil action, it may invoke the state secrets privilege in response to any allegation in any individual claim or counterclaim if the admission or denial by a party of that allegation in that individual claim or counterclaim would itself divulge a state secret to another party or the public. No adverse inference shall be drawn from a pleading of state secrets in an answer to an item in a complaint.

"(d) SUPPORTING AFFIDAVIT.—In each instance in which the United States invokes the state secrets privilege in response to 1 or more claims, it shall provide the court with an affidavit signed by the head of the executive branch agency with responsibility for, and control over, the state secrets involved explaining the factual basis for the privilege. The United States shall make public an unclassi fied version of the affidavit.

" 4054. Procedures for Determining Whether Evidence Is Protected from Disclosure by the State Secrets Privilege

"(a) INVOKING THE STATE SECRETS PRIVILEGE.— The United States may, in any civil action to which the United States is a party or in any other civil action before a Federal or State court, invoke the state secrets privilege as a ground for withholding information or evidence in discovery or for preventing the introduction of evidence at trial.

"(b) SUPPORTING AFFIDAVIT.—In each instance in which the United States invokes the state secrets privilege with respect to an item of information or evidence, the United States shall provide the court with an affidavit signed by the head of the executive branch agency with responsibility for, and control over, the state secrets involved explaining the factual basis for the claim of privilege. The United States shall make public an unclassified version of the affidavit.

"(c) HEARING.—A Federal court shall conduct a hearing to review any affidavit provided by the United States under this section and all evidence the United States asserts is protected from disclosure by the state secrets privilege.

"(d) REVIEW OF EVIDENCE.—

"(1) SUBMISSION OF EVIDENCE.—In addition to the affidavit provided under subsection (b), the United States shall make all evidence the United States claims is subject to the state secrets privilege available for the court to review, consistent with the requirements of section 4052, before any hearing conducted under this section.

"(2) INDEX OF MATERIALS.—The United States shall provide the court with a manageable index of evidence it contends is subject to the state secrets privilege by formulating a system ofitemizing and indexing that would correlate statements made in the affidavit provided under sub-section (b) with portions of the evidence the United States asserts is subject to the state secrets privilege. The index shall be specific enough to afford the court an adequate foundation to review the basis of the invocation of the privilege by the United States.

"(e) DETERMINATIONS AS TO APPLICABILITY OF STATE SECRETS PRIVILEGE.—

"(1) IN GENERAL.—As to each item of evidence that the United States asserts is protected by the state secrets privilege, the court shall review, consistent with the requirements of section 4052, the specific item of evidence to determine whether the claim of the United States is valid. Evidence is subject to the state secrets privilege if it contains a state secret, or there is no possible means of effectively segregating it from other evidence that contains a state secret.

"(2) ADMISSIBILITY.—If the court agrees that an item of evidence is subject to the state secrets privilege, that item shall not be disclosed or admissible as evidence.

"(3) DISCLOSURE.—If the court determines that an item of evidence is not subject to the state secrets privilege, the state secrets privilege does not prohibit the disclosure of that item to the opposing party or the admission of that item at trial, subject to the other rules of evidence.

"(f) NON-PRIVILEGED SUBSTITUTE.—If the court finds that material evidence is subject to the state secrets privilege and it is possible to craft a non-privileged sub- stitute for that privileged material evidence that provides a substantially equivalent opportunity to litigate the claim or defense as would that privileged material evidence, the court shall order the United States to provide such a substitute, which may consist of—

"(1) a summary of such privileged information;

"(2) a version of the evidence with privileged information redacted;

"(3) a statement admitting relevant facts that the privileged information would tend to prove; or

"(4) any other alternative as directed by the court in the interests of justice and protecting national security.

"(g) REFUSAL TO PROVIDE NON-PRIVILEGED SUBSTITUTE.—In a suit against the United States or an officer or agent of the Unites States acting in the official capacity of that officer or agent, if the court orders the United States to provide a non-privileged substitute for evidence in accordance with this section, and the United States fails to comply, the court shall resolve the disputed issue of fact or law to which the evidence pertains in the non-government party's favor.

“ 4055. Procedures When Evidence Protected by the State Secrets Privilege Is Necessary for Adjudication of a Claim or Counterclaim

“After reviewing all available evidence, privileged and non-privileged, a Federal court may dismiss a claim or counterclaim on the basis of the state secrets privilege only if the court determines that—

"(1) it is impossible to create for privileged material evidence a non-privileged substitute under section 4054(f) that provides a substantially equivalent opportunity to litigate the claim or counterclaim as would that privileged material evidence;

"(2) dismissal of the claim or counterclaim would not harm national security; and

"(3) continuing with litigation of the claim or counterclaim in the absence of the privileged material evidence would substantially impair the ability of a party to pursue a valid defense to the claim orcounterclaim.

“ 4056. Interlocutory Appeal

“(a) IN GENERAL.—The courts of appeal shall have jurisdiction of an appeal by any party from any interlocu tory decision or order of a district court of the United States under this chapter.

“(b) APPEAL.—

"(1) IN GENERAL.—An appeal taken under this section either before or during trial shall be expedited by the court of appeals.

"(2) DURING TRIAL.—If an appeal is taken during trial, the district court shall adjourn the trial until the appeal is resolved and the court of appeals—

"(A) shall hear argument on appeal as expeditiously as possible after adjournment of the trial by the district court;

"(B) may dispense with written briefs other than the supporting materials previously submitted to the trial court;

"(C) shall render its decision as expeditiously as possible after argument on appeal; and

"(D) may dispense with the issuance of a written opinion in rendering its decision.

" 4057. Security procedures

"(a) IN GENERAL.—The security procedures established under the Classified Information Procedures Act (18 U.S.C. App.) by the Chief Justice of the United States for the protection of classified information shall be used to protect against unauthorized disclosure of evidence protected by the state secrets privilege.

"(b) RULES.—The Chief Justice of the United States, in consultation with the Attorney General, the Director of National Intelligence, and the Secretary of Defense, may create additional rules or amend the rules to implement this chapter and shall submit any such additional rules or amendments to the Permanent Select Committee on Intelligence and the Committee on the Judiciary of the House of Representatives and the Select Committee on Intelligence and the Committee on the Judiciary of the Senate. Any such rules or amendments shall become effective 90 days after such submission, unless Congress provides otherwise. Rules and amendments shall comply with the letter and spirit of this chapter, and may include procedures concerning the role of magistrate judges and special masters in assisting courts in carrying out this chapter.

" 4058. Reporting

"(a) IN GENERAL.—The Attorney General shall report in writing to the Permanent Select Committee on Intelligence of the House of Representatives, the Select Committee on Intelligence of the Senate, and the chairmen and ranking minority members of the Committees on the Judiciary of the Senate and House of Representatives on any case in which the United States invokes the state secrets privilege, not later than 30 calendar days after the date of such assertion. Each report submitted under this subsection shall include all affidavits filed under this chapter by the United States.

"(b) OPERATION AND EFFECTIVENESS.—

"(1) IN GENERAL.—The Attorney General shall deliver to the committees of Congress described in subsection (a) a report concerning the operation and effectiveness of this chapter and including suggested amendments to this chapter.

"(2) DEADLINE.—The Attorney General shall submit a report under paragraph (1) not later than year after the date of enactment of this chapter, and every year there after until the date that is years after that date of enactment. After the date that is 3 years after that date of enactment, the Attorney General shall submit a report under paragraph (1) as necessary.

" 4059. Rule of Construction

"Nothing in this chapter is intended to supersede any other limit on the state secrets privilege under any other provision of law."

(b) TECHNICAL AND CONFORMING AMENDMENT.—The table of chapters for title 28, United States Code, is amended by adding at the end the following:

181. State secrets protection 4051

SEC. 3. APPLICATION TO PENDING CASES

The amendments made by this Act shall apply to any civil case pending on or after the date of enactment of this Act.

In: State Secrets Protection Act
Editor: Lara H. Nellington
ISBN 978-1-60692-711-3
© 2009 Nova Science Publishers, Inc.

Chapter 2

STATE SECRETS PROTECTION ACT*

I. BACKGROUND AND PURPOSE OF THE STATE SECRETS PROTECTION ACT#

A. Background and Need for the Legislation

The "state secrets privilege" is a common law rule of evidence that the Federal Government can invoke to prevent materials from being publicly disclosed in civil court proceedings, if the Government establishes that such disclosure would harm the Nation. In the early 1970s, Congress considered including a state secrets provision in the Federal Rules of Evidence, but it ultimately decided not to include any privileges [1]. Although numerous laws govern the handling of classified documents and other information that may implicate state secrets in specific contexts, the state secrets privilege has never been codified in statute.

The Supreme Court addressed the state secrets privilege at length for the first (and last) time in United States v. Reynolds, [2] a 1953 tort suit brought by widows of civilian engineers who died in an Air Force plane crash. The Reynolds decision has been criticized as internally contradictory and excessively deferential

* Excerpted from Senate Report 110-442 of 110TH CONGRESS REPORT 2d Session, dated August 1, 2008.

Mr. LEAHY, from the Committee on the Judiciary, submitted the following R E P O R T together with MINORITY VIEWS [To accompany S. 2533]. [Including cost estimate of the Congressional Budget Office]. The Committee on the Judiciary, to which was referred the bill (S. 2533), to enact a safe, fair, and responsible state secrets privilege Act, having considered the same, reports favorably thereon, with an amendment, and recommends that the bill, as amended, do pass.

to the Executive, [3] and commentators dispute the extent to which it is followed by lower courts today [4]. Nevertheless, it remains the foundational case on the privilege and the starting point for judicial review of privilege claims. As one commentator describes it, the analytical framework established in Reynolds comprises several basic principles:

> (a) the claim of privilege must be formally asserted by the head of the department charged with responsibility for the information; (b) the reviewing court has the ultimate responsibility to determine whether disclosure of the information in issue would pose a "reasonable danger'' to national security; (c) the court should calibrate the extent of deference it gives to the Executive's assertion with regard to the plaintiff's need for access to the information; (d) the court can personally review the sensitive information on an in camera, ex parte basis if necessary; and (e) once the privilege is found to attach, it is absolute and cannot be overcome by a showing of need or offsetting considerations [5].

In recent years, the executive branch has asserted the privilege more frequently and broadly than before, typically to seek dismissal of lawsuits at the pleadings stage [6]. Facing allegations of unlawful Government conduct ranging from domestic warrantless surveillance, [7] to employment discrimination, [8] to retaliation against whistleblowers, [9] to torture and "extraordinary rendition," [10] the Bush-Cheney administration has invoked the privilege in an effort to shut down civil suits against both Government officials and private parties. Courts have largely acquiesced. While there is some debate over the extent to which this represents a quantitative or qualitative break from past practice, "[w]hat is undebatable *** is that the privilege is currently being invoked as grounds for dismissal of entire categories of cases challenging the constitutionality of Government action," [11] and that a strong public perception has emerged that sees the privilege as a tool for Executive abuse. The state secrets privilege "has long been the subject of academic criti cism," [12] but the criticism has escalated dramatically and aroused widespread concern. Indeed, in the burgeoning literature on the privilege, it is hard to find a single positive view on the current state of the law [13]

One line of criticism has emphasized the lack of uniformity in judicial review of privilege claims, and the confusion and uncertainty this invites. For several decades, Congress has provided procedures to govern the use of sensitive national security evidence under the Classified Information Procedures Act ("CIPA"), [14] the Freedom of Information Act ("FOIA"), [15] and the Foreign Intelligence Surveillance Act ("FISA") [16] Yet, with only a single ambiguous Supreme Court decision from the 1950s to guide them, [17] lower courts have been taking disparate approaches when faced with a claim of the state secrets privilege. The Supreme Court has declined to intervene [18]. As a result, the courts have reached inconsistent results, and litigants have been left to "flounder under the ad hoc procedures and varying standards employed by the courts today." [19].

Furthermore, some Federal courts have viewed assertions of the privilege as a virtual "automatic win" for the Government. Courts have refused to review key pieces of allegedly privileged evidence, given unwarranted deference to the executive branch on the danger of disclosure, upheld claims of state secrets even when the purported secrets were publicly available, and dismissed lawsuits at the pleadings stage, without considering any evidence at all.20 Scholars have found that courts have required in camera inspection of allegedly privileged documents in fewer than one-third of the reported cases in which the privilege has been invoked, and that this proportion is declining [21]. As a result, "even though the Reynolds case held that 'judicial control over the evidence in a case cannot be abdicated to the caprice of executive officers,' the practical effect of the decision [has been] to cause precisely that result." [22] When courts fail to scrutinize assertions of the privilege, they leave open the possibility that the privilege will be used to cover up Government wrongdoing, thereby denying justice to litigants and giving the executive branch the ability to violate statutes and constitutional rights with impunity.

The pitfalls of such extreme deference to the executive branch can be seen in United States v. Reynolds, [23] the very case that serves as the basis for privilege doctrine to this day. In Reynolds, the widows of the deceased B–29 crew members asked to see the Government's accident report. Citing the state secrets privilege, the Government refused to turn it over. The Supreme Court accepted the executive branch's assertion that the accident report contained references to secret electronic equipment and refused to allow the report to be considered as evidence, without ever looking at the report itself.

When the accident report was declassified in the 1990s, it turned out that it did not contain any references to secret electronic equipment—but it did contain embarrassing information revealing Government negligence (that the plane lacked standard safeguards to prevent the engine from overheating) [24]. The notion that the entire report constituted a state secret was thrown into serious doubt. As summarized by Louis Fisher, Specialist in Constitutional Law at the Library of Congress and the leading expert on the Reynolds case: "Instead [of looking at the disputed documents], the Court relied entirely on assertions by executive officials about the content of the documents. We now know, by looking at the documents, that they contain no state secrets. The Court was misled by the executive branch and allowed itself to be misled" [25].

As use of the privilege has expanded and criticism has grown, public confidence has suffered. Mistrust of the privilege breeds cynicism and suspicion about the national security activities of the U.S. Government, and it causes Americans to lose respect for the notion of legitimate state secrets. Perversely, overuse of the privilege may undermine national security by making those with access to sensitive information more likely to release it. As one former CIA officer stated recently: "There will finally be an instance where you've cried 'state secrets' so many times that [no one will] believe it anymore, and potentially something that is a state secret will get out" [26]

In response to these concerns, many have called on Congress to provide guidance to the judiciary and the executive branch on use of the privilege. The American Bar Association issued a report "urg[ing] Congress to enact legislation governing federal civil cases implicating the state secrets privilege." [27] The bipartisan Constitution Project found that "legislative action [on the privilege] is essential to restore and strengthen the basic rights and liberties provided by our constitutional system of government" [28]. A letter on the privilege sent to Congress by leading constitutional scholars concluded that there "is a need for new rules designed to protect the system of checks and balances, individual rights, national security, fairness in the courtroom, and the adversary process" [29]. Patricia M. Wald, former Chief Judge of the D.C. Circuit, testified that "[t]here is a wide consensus in the legal community" that Congress should prescribe regulations on the privilege, and that "[t]he time is now ripe for such legislation"[30].

Courts and scholars have debated the origins of the privilege [31] and whether it is a "mere" common law rule or whether it also has some foundation in the Constitution, notwithstanding the lack of explicit textual or historical support for such a view [32] Regardless of whether the privilege has any constitutional dimension, however, there is widespread agreement that Congress has constitutional authority to regulate the privilege, [33] based on its Article III powers to set rules of procedure and evidence for the Federal courts, [34] its Article I powers related to national security and foreign affairs, [35] and the Necessary and Proper Clause [36]. Article II is not the only relevant part of the Constitution. Even if the state secrets privilege were in some respect "rooted" in our constitutional structure, [37] there is no bar to Congress, using its own authorities rooted in the Constitution, exercising concurrent authority over the protection of state secrets or providing rules for implementation of the privilege. Congress has passed numerous statutes regulating judicial proceedings that deal with national security information, such as the Classified Information Procedures

Act, the Freedom of Information Act, and the Foreign Intelligence Surveillance Act, none of which has ever faced a successful constitutional challenge [38].

In response to the growing concerns about the state secrets privilege, Senator Kennedy, Senator Specter, and Senator Leahy introduced the State Secrets Protection Act to provide a systematic approach to the privilege and thereby bring stability, predictability, and clarity to this area of the law and restore the public trust in Government and the courts. In introducing the bill, Senator Kennedy remarked:

> [In recent years], use of the state secrets privilege has dramatically increased—and the harmful consequences of its irregular application by courts have become painfully clear.
>
> Injured plaintiffs have been denied justice; courts have failed to address fundamental questions of constitutional rights and separation of powers; and confusion pervades this area of law. The Senate debate on reforming the Foreign Intelligence Surveillance Act has become far more difficult than it ought to be, because many believe that if courts hear lawsuits against telecommunications companies, the courts will be unable to deal fairly and effectively with the Government's invocation of the privilege.
>
> Studies show that the Bush administration has raised the privilege in over 25% more cases per year than previous administrations, and has sought dismissal in over 90% more cases. As one scholar recently noted, this administration has used the privilege to "seek blanket dismissal of every case challenging the constitutionality of specific, ongoing government programs" related to its war on terrorism, and as a result, the privilege is impairing the ability of Congress and the judiciary to perform their constitutional duty to check Executive power.
>
> Another leading scholar recently found that "in practical terms, the state secrets privilege never fails." Like other commentators, he concluded that "the state secrets privilege is the most powerful secrecy privilege available to the president," and "the people of the United States have suffered needlessly because the law is now a servant to executive claims of national security."
>
> In 1980, Congress enacted the Classified Information Procedures Act (CIPA) to provide Federal courts with clear statutory guidance on handling secret evidence in criminal cases. For almost 30 years, courts have effectively applied that law to make criminal trials fairer and safer. During that period, Congress has also regulated judicial review of national security materials under the Foreign Intelligence Surveillance Act and the Freedom of Information Act. Because of these laws, Federal judges regularly review and handle highly classified evidence in many types of cases.
>
> Yet in civil cases, litigants have been left behind. Congress has failed to provide clear rules or standards for determining whether evidence is protected by the state secrets privilege. We've failed to develop procedures that will protect

injured parties and also prevent the disclosure of sensitive information. Because use of the state secrets privilege has escalated in recent years, there's an increasing need for the judiciary and the Executive to have clear, fair, and safe rules [39].

On the same occasion, Senator Specter remarked:

Senator Kennedy and I are introducing this bipartisan bill in order to harmonize the law applicable in cases involving the executive branch's invocation of the privilege. This bill is timely for several reasons. First, the use of the privilege appears to be on the rise in the post-September 11, 2001, era, which has generated new public attention and concern about its legitimacy. Second, there is some disparity among the district and appellate court opinions analyzing the privilege, particularly as to the question of whether courts must independently review the allegedly privileged evidence. Finally, a codified test for evaluating state secrets that requires courts to review the evidence in camera—a Latin phrase meaning "in the judge's private chambers"—will help to reassure the public that the claims are neither spurious nor intended to cover up alleged Government misconduct. With greater checks and balances and greater accountability, there is a commensurate increase in public confidence in our institutions of Government.

In view of its increasing use, inconsistent application, and public criticism, we think the time is ripe to pass legislation codifying standards on the state secrets privilege. Our bill builds upon proposals by the American Bar Association and legal scholars who have called upon Congress to legislate in this area [40].

At the Judiciary Committee's hearing on the state secrets privilege, in his opening statement, Chairman Leahy noted:

> The state secrets privilege has been used in recent years to stymie litigation at its very inception in cases alleging egregious Government misconduct, such as extraordinary rendition and warrantless eavesdropping on the communications of American citizens. Reflecting on recent state secrets litigation, The New York Times has observed: "To avoid accountability, [the Bush] administration has repeatedly sought early dismissal of lawsuits that might finally expose government misconduct, brandishing flimsy claims that going forward would put national security secrets at risk."
>
> The clearest example of the state secrets privilege short- circuiting litigation is the 2006 case of Khaled El-Masri. Mr. El-Masri, a German citizen of Lebanese descent, alleged that he was kidnapped on New Year's Eve in 2003 in Macedonia, and transported against his will to Afghanistan, where he was detained and tortured as part of the Bush administration's extraordinary rendition program. He sued the Government over his alleged detention and harsh

> treatment. A district court judge in Virginia dismissed the entire lawsuit on the basis of an ex parte declaration from the Director of the CIA and despite the fact that the Government has admitted that the rendition program exists. Mr. El-Masri has no other remedy. Our justice system is off limits to him, and no judge ever reviewed any of the actual evidence.
>
> The Government has also asserted the state secrets privilege in the litigation over the warrantless wiretapping of Americans that took place for more than five years. There, a district court judge has rejected the Government's claim that the very subject matter at issue was a state secret, but the Government is appealing.
>
> The state secrets privilege serves important goals where properly invoked. But there are serious consequences for litigants and for the American public when the privilege is used to terminate litigation alleging serious Government misconduct. For the aggrieved parties, it means that the courthouse doors are closed—forever—regardless of the severity of their injury. They will never have their day in court. For the American public, it means less accountability, because there will be no judicial scrutiny of improper actions of the Executive, and no check or balance.

Secrecy can be important to national security, but it can also deprive the American people of their ability to judge the effectiveness of their Government on national security matters. It is critical that Federal judges not abdicate their role in our system of checks and balances as a check on the Executive [41].

B. Legislative Intent

The State Secrets Protection Act allows the United States to preserve its commitment to constitutional rights and the rule of law, without compromising its national defense or foreign policy objectives. Rather than invent new tools or procedures for Federal courts in reviewing claims of the state secrets privilege, the bill draws on existing practices to make judicial review more regular and more rigorous—and to protect all legitimate state secrets. As the original co-sponsors of the bill explained in a letter to Senate colleagues:

> The [State Secrets Protection] Act recognizes that state secrets must be protected, and it enables the executive branch to avoid publicly revealing evidence if doing so might disclose a state secret. Secure judicial proceedings and other safeguards that have proven effective under CIPA and the Freedom of Information Act will ensure that the litigation does not reveal state secrets.

> At the same time, the State Secrets Protection Act will prevent the executive branch from using the privilege to deny parties their day in court or shield illegal activity that is not actually sensitive * * *.
>
> The State Secrets Protection Act requires courts to consider evidence for which the privilege is claimed, in order to determine whether the executive branch has validly invoked the privilege. It gives parties an opportunity to make a preliminary case with their own evidence before a lawsuit is dismissed, and it allows courts to develop solutions to let lawsuits proceed, such as directing the Government to produce non-privileged substitutes for secret evidence. Many of these powers are already available to courts, but they often go unused.
>
> The Act also draws on CIPA to include provisions for congressional oversight and expedited interlocutory appeal [42]

In prescribing rules for judicial review of the state secrets privilege, the bill seeks to accomplish the following general goals:

- The bill provides a uniform set of procedures for Federal courts faced with assertions of the state secrets privilege, promoting clarity, predictability, and fairness in judicial review of these claims.
- The bill codifies many of the best practices that are already available to courts but that often go unused, such as in camera hearings, non-privileged substitutes, and special masters.
- The bill requires judges to look at the evidence that the Government claim is privileged, rather than rely solely on Government affidavits, so that the privilege is not abused by the executive branch to cover up information that is not actually sensitive.

  The bill forbids judges from dismissing cases at the pleadings stage on the basis of the privilege. This makes clear that the state secrets privilege is an evidentiary rule, not a justiciability rule, and can only be asserted with respect to items of evidence that plain-tiffs seek in discovery or intend to disclose in litigation. At the same time, the bill protects innocent defendants by allowing cases to be dismissed when privileged evidence would be needed to establish a valid defense.
- The bill gives plaintiffs a chance to make a preliminary case using evidence they have gathered on their own.
- The bill preserves the adversarial process—and the truth-seeking function of that process—to the fullest extent possible consistent with the protection of national security.

- The bill instructs courts to order the Government to produce non-privileged substitutes for privileged evidence, when this is possible, to allow cases to go forward safely.
- The bill instructs courts to avoid excessively deferential standards of review and to retain full control over privilege determinations. This approach rejects a line of judicial precedent that applies "utmost deference" to the executive branch; the Government's assertions deserve weight and respect, but they do not deserve a reprieve from the rigorous, independent judicial scrutiny demanded by our adjudicatory system.
- The bill puts in place numerous security procedures, including closed hearings, security clearance requirements, and sealed orders, to ensure that secrets do not leak out during litigation.
- The bill sets reporting requirements to ensure that Congress stays informed on use of the privilege and can take corrective action if necessary.
- The bill solves the crisis of legitimacy currently surrounding the privilege, by setting clear rules that take into account both constitutional and policy considerations.
- The judicial review procedures set forth in the bill to accomplish these goals are discussed in detail below. The major steps in the process may be summarized as follows:
- The Government may assert the privilege to withhold information in discovery or to prevent the disclosure of information in litigation. The assertion is made through an affidavit signed by the head of the relevant agency and submitted to the court. An unclassified version of the affidavit must be made public.
- The Government must then submit the evidence (or, in certain situations, a sampling of the evidence) to the court for in camera review, along with a document index to facilitate the review.
- The court holds a hearing to assist in its examination of the evidence and to determine the validity of the state secrets claim. The hearing shall be conducted in camera unless the only issues to be determined are issues of law, and a public hearing would not risk disclosure of state secrets. Based upon its prior review of the evidence, the court determines whether to conduct the hearing ex parte as well as in camera. The hearing may be conducted ex parte only if the court determines that the interests of justice and national security cannot adequately be protected through less restrictive measures, including limiting attendance at the hearing to attorneys

with appropriate security clearances, appointing a guardian ad litem with the necessary security clearance, or issuing protective orders.

- The court may appoint a special master or other independent advisor to assist it in understanding the evidence and arguments and in determining whether the evidence is privileged If the court determines that evidence is privileged, the evidence itself may not be disclosed. However, if the court determines that it is possible for the Government to craft a non-privileged substitute for the evidence, the court shall order the Government to do so. If the Government refuses, the court shall resolve the disputed issue of fact or law to which the evidence pertains in the non-Government party's favor.
- After issuing its determination on all claims of privilege and reviewing all pertinent evidence, the court may dismiss the case or claim on the basis of the state secrets privilege only if it determines that it would be impossible to proceed fairly with a non-privileged substitute for the privileged evidence, dismissal will not harm national security, and disclosure of the privileged evidence would be necessary to the pursuit of a valid defense.
- The court's determinations shall be subject to interlocutory appeal.

II. History of the Bill and Committee Consideration

A. Introduction of the Bill

Senators Kennedy, Specter and Leahy introduced S. 2533, the State Secrets Protection Act, on January 22, 2007. The bill was referred to the Committee on the Judiciary. Since the bill's introduction and prior to its Committee consideration, Senators Feingold, Whitehouse, Webb, Clinton, Dodd, McCaskill, Schumer, and Biden joined as cosponsors.

B. Committee Consideration

On February 13, 2008, Chairman Leahy chaired a Committee hearing on "Examining the State Secrets Privilege: Protecting National Security While Preserving Accountability." Testifying on Panel I was Carl J. Nichols, Deputy Assistant Attorney General, U.S. Department of Justice, Civil Division. Testifying on Panel II were the Honorable Patricia M. Wald, former Chief Judge, U.S. Court of Appeals for the D.C. Circuit; Louis Fisher, Specialist in Constitutional Law, Law Library of the Library of Congress; Robert M. Chesney, Associate Professor, Wake Forest University School of Law; and Michael Vatis, Partner, Steptoe & Johnson LLP. In addition to the prepared statements of the witnesses, the following materials were submitted for the record: October 4, 2007 letter to Congress by 23 scholars of constitutional law; May 31, 2007 statement of the Constitution Project's Liberty and Security Committee & Coalition to Defend Checks and Balances on "Reforming the State Secrets Privilege"; August 2007 report on state secrets legislation by the American Bar Association Section of Individual Rights and Responsibilities and the Association of the Bar of the City of New York; prepared statement of H. Thomas Wells, Jr., President-Elect, submitted on behalf of the American Bar Association; statement of William H. Webster, former Judge, U.S. District Court for the Eastern District of Missouri, Judge, U.S. Court of Appeals for the Eighth Circuit, Director, Federal Bureau of Investigation, and Director of Central Intelligence; February 8, 2008 letter to Senator Kennedy from William G. Weaver, Associate Professor, University of Texas at El Paso, and Danielle Escontrias; prepared statement of Patricia Reynolds Herring; prepared statement of Susan Parker Brauner.

The bill was placed on the Committee's agenda for consideration on February 28, 2008. On April 24, 2008, the Committee on the Judiciary considered S. 2533 [43]. Senator Leahy offered a Managers' amendment, in the nature of a complete substitute, which was adopted by unanimous consent. This amendment made a number of changes to clarify the use of security clearances, hearings, congressional reporting, and other provisions in the bill.

Senator Feinstein offered an amendment to provide a standard of review for judges in evaluating assertions of the state secrets privilege. This amendment was accepted on a rollcall vote. The vote record is as follows:

TALLY: 18 YEAS, 1 NAY

Yeas (18): Biden (D–DE), Brownback (R–KS), Cardin (D–MD), Coburn (R–OK), Cornyn (R–TX), Durbin (D–IL), Feingold (D–WI), Feinstein (D–CA), Graham (R–SC), Grassley (R–IA), Hatch (R–UT), Kennedy, (D–MA), Kohl (D–WI), Kyl (R–AZ), Leahy (D–VT), Schumer (D–NY), Sessions (R–AL), Whitehouse (D–RI).

Nays (1): Specter (R–PA).

Senator Hatch offered an amendment to strike the provisions in the bill relating to attorney security clearances. The amendment was rejected on a rollcall vote. The vote record is as follows:

TALLY: 8 YEAS, 10 NAYS, 1 PASS

Yeas (8): Brownback (R–KS), Coburn (R–OK), Cornyn (R–TX), Hatch (R–UT), Kyl (R–AZ), Graham (R–SC), Grassley (R–IA), Sessions (R–AL).

Nays (10): Biden (D–DE), Cardin (D–MD), Durbin (D–IL), Fein- gold (D–WI), Feinstein (D–CA), Kennedy (D–MA), Kohl (D–WI), Leahy (D–VT), Schumer (D–NY), Whitehouse (D–RI).

Pass (1): Specter (R–PA).

The Committee then voted to report the State Secrets Protection Act, as amended, favorably to the Senate. The Committee proceeded by rollcall vote as follows:

TALLY: 11 YEAS, 8 NAYS

Yeas (11): Biden (D–DE), Cardin (D–MD), Durbin (D–IL), Fein- gold (D–WI), Feinstein (D–CA), Kennedy (D–MA), Kohl (D–WI), Leahy (D–VT), Schumer (D–NY), Specter (R–PA), Whitehouse (D– RI).

Nays (8): Brownback (R–KS), Coburn (R–OK), Cornyn (R–TX), Hatch (R–UT), Kyl (R–AZ), Graham (R–SC), Grassley (R–IA), Sessions (R–AL).

III. Section-by-Section Summary of the Bill

Section 1. Short Title

This section cites the short title of the bill as the "State Secrets Protection Act."

Section 2. State Secrets Protection

This section adds nine sections to title 28 of the United States Code, as follows.

Section 4051. In a new section 4051 of the United States Code, the bill sets forth definitions.

First, this section defines “evidence” under the bill as “any document, witness testimony, discovery response, affidavit, object, or other material” that could be admissible or discoverable in court under the Federal rules of evidence or civil procedure. “Evidence” is given this broad definition to ensure that the state secrets privilege protects sensitive information from public disclosure at every stage in the litigation process. Coupled with the provisions in the bill tying the state secrets privilege to “evidence,” this definition also makes clear that the privilege applies only to items that might be discoverable or admissible, and does not apply to abstract concepts, ideas, or assertions or to general facts.

Second, this section defines a “state secret” as “any information that, if disclosed publicly, would be reasonably likely to cause significant harm to the national defense or foreign relations of the United States.” The sponsors of the legislation believe it is important to set a definition of “state secret,” so that all courts will evaluate claims of the state secrets privilege from an identical starting point.

The bill’s definition of “state secret” is intentionally broad, in that it covers both national defense and foreign relations and applies the same standard to both. However, the definition does not include information that is already available to the public or that has only a remote chance of causing harm. Information that is already public should not qualify as a state secret because its disclosure through the litigation process would not reveal new facts or insights, and thus would not be reasonably likely to cause significant harm. “Public” disclosure does not encompass the disclosure of information in the context of the proceedings set forth in the bill; the bill requires the executive branch to make evidence available to the court precisely so that the court can determine whether public disclosure, to the world at large, would be appropriate. The state secrets privilege, as defined in this section, does not necessarily apply to every item of classified information; but that does not mean the information is “de-classified.” Classified materials not found to qualify as state secrets will still be subject to the ordinary rules governing the disclosure of classified information in civil litigation and in other settings [44].

The requirements of reasonable likelihood and significant harm present the court with two distinct inquiries in evaluating whether information qualifies as a state secret, one focused on the probability of harm and the other on magnitude of harm. The probability threshold is needed so that speculative or unlikely risks do not trigger the privilege. The magnitude threshold is needed so that insignificant harms do not trigger it. “Reasonably likely’’ and “significant harm’’ are the standards recommended by many experts in this area of law, including the American Bar Association, which had input from the Association's criminal and national security units. In today's globalized world, almost anything can be argued to cause potential harm to the national defense or foreign relations, and improbable or insignificant harms should not be the basis for withholding evidence that may be critical for the accuracy and integrity of litigation. Tests for probability and magnitude are needed as a check against overly expansive executive branch characterizations of national defense and foreign relations interests.

The Supreme Court never clearly defined "state secret'' in United States v. Reynolds or in subsequent cases, but it suggested in Reynolds that "the occasion for the privilege is appropriate'' when the Government "satisf[ies] the court, from all the circumstances of the case, that there is a reasonable danger that compulsion of the evidence will expose military matters which, in the interest of national security, should not be divulged.'' [45] Many courts have followed Reynolds in adopting this definition, but some courts have used other formulations, for example, that the privilege allows the Government to withhold information from discovery when disclosure would be "inimical to the national security,'' [46] would "jeopardize national security,'' [47] or would "adversely affect national security.''[48]

The definition of "state secret'' used in the bill is preferable (although fundamentally similar) to the Reynolds formulation for two main reasons [49]. First, the definition in the bill is more precise. It avoids the vague language of Reynolds about "matters which, in the interest of national security, should not be divulged," and focuses the judicial inquiry on the likelihood and severity of the potential harm at issue.

Second, the definition in the bill expressly includes "foreign relations," whereas the Reynolds language does not. Some courts have stated that the privilege protects both foreign relations and national security interests [50] — which makes sense as a matter of policy and in light of the executive branch's constitutional responsibilities in both areas—and the bill codifies that understanding. The sponsors of the legislation assume that the standard of "significant harm" will generally be more difficult to meet with respect to foreign relations as compared to the national defense, and routine matters involving international trade, diplomatic relations, or the United States' image in the world should not qualify. Yet in some rare instances, the court may find that the likely impact of disclosure on foreign relations would be sufficiently grave, in terms of the national interest, as to threaten "significant harm" on the order of disclosure of sensitive security information.

Section 4052. In a new section 4052 of the United States Code, the bill sets forth rules governing procedures related to this chapter.

This section instructs the court in determining who shall have access to documents and proceedings under the Act. It provides guidance on when hearings may be in camera and ex parte, when participation in hearings and access to documents may be conditioned on security clearances, when protective orders may be issued, and when opinions or orders may be issued under seal or in redacted form. It also advises the court that it may appoint a special master or other independent advisor. In the use of all of these procedural measures, the bill is clear that it is the court, not the executive branch, that determines whether and in what ways the measures will be applied.

Subsection 4052(a) instructs the court to determine which filings, motions, and affidavits, or portions thereof, shall be submitted ex parte, and it affirms the court's authority to order redacted, unclassified, or summary substitutes of evidence as appropriate. The requirement in § 4052(a)(3) that the court "tak[e] into consideration the interests of justice and national security" establishes general principles to guide these determinations. The interests of justice include fairness, due process, and instrumental rationality. Although depriving litigants of full access to the Government's filings, motions, and affidavits may be necessary in some instances to protect the interests of national security, it can disserve the interests of justice that underlie our adversarial system by impairing the abil- ity of litigants to argue their case. Courts must be mindful of both interests.

Subsection 4052(b) sets a requirement that all hearings based on the assertion of the state secrets privilege, as provided for in subsection 4054(c), be conducted in camera, except if the court determines that the hearing relates only to a question of law and does not present a risk of revealing state secrets, in which case the hearing shall not be conducted in camera. In the hearings referenced in subsection 4052(b)(1)(A), the court reviews the allegedly privileged evidence and takes argument to inform its determination on whether and to what extent that evidence deserves special protection. Given that the purpose of these hearings is to test state secrets claims, it makes sense from a national security standpoint to have the hearings be closed to the public [51].

Subsection 4052(b)(2) allows the hearings, or portions thereof, to be conducted ex parte as well as in camera, "if the court determines, following in camera review of the evidence, that the interests of justice and national security cannot adequately be protected through the [security clearance requirements and protective orders] described in subsection (c) and (d)." This provision recognizes the possibility that nothing short of ex parte hearings will adequately protect the interests of national security in certain instances. However, this provision also recognizes that as a general matter, the interests of justice, the truth-seeking function of the court, and reasoned decisionmaking are best served through the adversarial process, and that shutting out non-governmental parties from hearings is an extreme measure. As indicated by the reference to alternative measures described in subsections (c) and (d) and by the invocation of "the interests of justice," ex parte hearings are meant to be a measure of last resort. The court's prior in camera review of the evidence will enable it to make an informed decision as to whether ex parte proceedings are necessary.

Subsection 4052(c) requires the court to limit participation in hearings on the state secrets privilege to attorneys with appropriate security clearances, if the executive branch makes such a request and the court "determines that limiting participation in that manner would serve the interests of national security." Under the structure of the bill, hearings play a central role as the forum in which litigants can present arguments to the court about why information does or does not qualify for the state secrets privilege. If at all possible, litigants and their attorneys should be present at the hearing to enable full adversarial testing of the executive branch's assertions, and the delay and the burden associated with clearance procedures should be avoided. However, this subsection recognizes that protecting national security may require the court in some cases to limit attendance at the hearing, or portions thereof, to cleared attorneys. Protective orders, § 4052(d), and sealed or redacted orders, § 4052(e), are likewise permissible but disfavored.

In a situation in which a litigant's attorney is barred from participating in a state secrets pre-trial hearing for national security reasons, subsection 4054(c)(1) authorizes the court to appoint a guardian ad litem with the necessary security clearances to represent that litigant. Although the right to employ the attorney of one's choosing is an important tenet of our civil justice system, guardians ad litem offer a second-best solution for those portions of proceedings from which one's attorney is excluded. Guardians ad litem can ensure that a litigant's interests and arguments are represented in these hearings, and thereby preserve a significant measure of adversariality in the privilege review process.

Because the process of obtaining a clearance may take time, subsection 4052(c)(2) allows the court to suspend proceedings during the duration of this process if doing so would serve the interests of justice. In recognition of the possibility that the executive branch could use the security clearance process as a delaying tactic or as a means to disqualify attorneys who are otherwise deserving of clearance, subsection 4054(c)(3) authorizes the court "to review in camera and ex parte the reasons of the United States for denying or delaying the clearance to ensure that the United States is not withholding a security clearance from a particular attorney or class of attorneys for any reason other than protection of national security." This provision does not grant the court any authority to issue a security clearance or to require the Government to do so; rather, it clarifies that the Government may not abuse the security clearance process in an effort to undermine the bill. If the court determines that the Government is delaying or denying a security clearance for reasons other than the protection of national security, it may exercise its equitable authority to sanction the Government in an appropriate manner, while appointing an individual who has or can obtain the necessary clearance as a guardian ad litem to represent the plaintiff.

Subsection 4052(f) authorizes the court to appoint a special master or other independent advisor who holds the necessary security clearances, to the extent any are needed, to assist the court in handling any matter under the bill. Federal judges already have legal authority to appoint independent experts to assess Government secrecy claims, [52] and though they rarely avail themselves of this authority, experience shows it can be used "with great success" [53]. Special masters offer judges a tool to make their review of materials less burdensome and more informed, and to help judges better understand the factual predicates and policy judgments involved in executive branch claims regarding national defense or foreign rela- tions. Subsection 4052(f) is meant to stimulate courts to use special masters.

Section 4053. In a new section 4053 of the United States Code, the bill sets forth procedures for answering a complaint.

This section sets rules for the executive branch in asserting the state secrets privilege when answering a complaint or intervening in a civil action.

Subsection 4053(a) allows the Government to intervene in any civil action to assert the privilege, which represents no change from current practice.

Subsection 4053(b) clarifies that the court is prohibited from dismissing cases or claims on state secrets grounds except as provided under section 4055 of the bill. This subsection also clarifies that the court may not rule on a motion to dismiss or for summary judgment until after completion of hearings under subsection 4054(c), except when such ruling can be made entirely independently of the Government's assertion of the privilege. Hence, the court may not dismiss a case or claim on state secrets grounds at the pleadings stage; it may dismiss a case or claim on state secrets grounds only after any allegedly privileged evidence has been identified in the course of discovery or pre-trial proceedings and the court has ruled on the assertions of the privilege. Furthermore, if a plaintiff's ability to survive summary judgment may depend on whether the plaintiff is able to discover or introduce evidence that the Government asserts is privileged, the court must rule on the assertion of privilege before deciding the summary judgment motion. The rationale for this provision is set forth in the discussion of section 4055, below.

Subsection 4053(c) allows the executive branch to plead the state secrets privilege in response to any allegation in any individual claim or counterclaim and, in so doing, to avoid admitting or denying certain facts or having the court draw an adverse inference or admission. By allowing the Government to plead "state secrets" in such a manner, the bill enables lawsuits to move forward without risk that the Government's answer will itself reveal state secrets. The requirement that the Government plead the privilege in response to allegations, rather than to claims or counterclaims, imposes a burden of specificity on the Government to tailor its assertions of the privilege to particular allegations that the Government believes implicate state secrets.

Subsection 4053(d) requires the executive branch, when it pleads the state secrets privilege, to explain its factual basis for doing so in an affidavit signed by the relevant agency head. This explanation will help the court, when reviewing the evidence, to evaluate the persuasiveness of the Government's claimed need for the privilege. The non-delegation language used in this subsection is based on language from United States v. Reynolds, which stated that for the Government to assert the state secrets privilege, "[t]here must be formal claim of privilege, lodged by the head of the department which has control over the matter, after actual personal consideration by that officer"[54].

Section 4054. In a new section 4054 of the United States Code, the bill sets forth procedures for determining whether evidence is protected from disclosure by the state secrets privilege.

This section establishes procedures for courts to follow in determining the applicability of the state secrets privilege. It requires the court to hold a hearing to examine the evidence and affidavits and to rule on the Government's assertion of the privilege. The Government must make all evidence it claims is subject to the privilege available for the court to review; this must be done prior to the hearing, so that the court can determine whether to conduct the hearing ex parte or take other protective measures. The Government must also provide a manageable index of the evidence.

If the court finds that an item of evidence contains a state secret, or there is no possible means of effectively segregating it from other evidence that contains a state secret, then that item is privileged and may not be disclosed. In determining whether public disclosure of an item of evidence would be reasonably likely to cause significant harm, the court shall give substantial weight to the views of the United States, and shall weigh the testimony of a Government expert in the same manner as, and along with, any other expert testimony. When material evidence is found to be privileged, the court must, if possible, order the Government to create a non- privileged substitute for the evidence, such as an unclassified summary or a redacted version. If the Government refuses to turn over evidence or to provide a non-privileged substitute ordered by the court, the court will resolve the relevant issue of fact or law against the Government.

Subsection 4054(a) provides that the United States may assert the state secrets privilege in any civil action as a ground for preventing the public disclosure of evidence. This subsection acknowledges that United States may assert the privilege in State court as well as Federal court, which is no change from current practice, although the judicial procedures established by the bill apply only to Federal courts.

Echoing subsection 4053(d), subsection 4054(b) requires the executive branch, when it asserts the state secrets privilege, to explain its factual basis for doing so in an affidavit signed by the relevant agency head. This subsection also requires the executive branch to make public an unclassified version of this affidavit, so that the American people can see its arguments. The unclassified version should contain as much detail as the Government can provide without compromising national security or disclosing the alleged state secrets themselves. In many cases, this should be achievable simply by redacting names, operational details, or similar information.

Subsection 4054(c) requires the court to hold a pre-trial hearing or hearings (i) to examine the items of evidence that the Government asserts are subject to the state secrets privilege, (ii) to examine the affidavits submitted by the Government in support of its assertions of the privilege, and (iii) to determine the validity of any assertions of the privilege. These hearings must be "consistent with the requirements of section 4052." Therefore, they must comply with subsection 4052(b)(2)'s limitations on ex parte proceedings, and they must be in camera unless they relate only to a question of law and do not present a risk of revealing state secrets The central role assigned by the bill to these hearings reflects the intent to make judicial review of privilege claims as careful, thorough, and adversarial as possible, consistent with national security. Through the participation of counsel and/or guardians ad litem, the Government's legal and factual assertions relating to its claim of the privilege may be challenged and developed before the court, helping the court to understand better the allegedly privileged evidence and the likely significance of ordering its public disclosure. Litigants will have the opportunity to explain why they believe evidence should or should not be found privileged or relevant. There is some precedent for this use of pre-trial hearings in CIPA [55].

At the same time, pre-trial hearings under subsection 4054(c) are not meant to be overly burdensome. If there are questions regarding the relevance or admissibility of evidence, the court should address those questions at the outset of the hearing; if the court determines that the evidence is irrelevant or inadmissible, the privilege issue will become moot, and there will be no need to proceed further with the hearing. Moreover, the court need not pore over every item of evidence and rule on each item's privileged status during the hearing itself. The hearings are a means to inform, rationalize, and enhance the court's review of, and decision-making on, allegedly privileged evidence, but they need not be the forum in which all such review and decision making takes place.

Subsection 4054(d)(1) requires the United States to "make all evidence [it] claims is subject to the state secrets privilege available for the court to review, consistent with the requirements of section 4052, before any hearing conducted under this section." This provision enables the court to determine whether it is appropriate to impose any restrictions on the non-Government party's participation in the hearing; it also ensures that the court will be able to make the most effective use of the hearing for its consideration of the allegedly privileged evidence. Although the executive branch must make all allegedly privileged evidence "available for the court to review" before any hearing, the court may in appropriate cases avail itself of sampling under subsection 4054(d)(2).

Subsection 4054(d)(2) authorizes the court to review "a sufficient sampling of the [allegedly privileged] evidence," rather than each item of evidence, if it determines that certain specified conditions are met. This sampling provision is meant to preserve judicial economy in cases in which there is no cost to doing so, but it is not meant to change in any way the qualitative nature of the court's review. Sampling should not be a routine occurrence. It should be invoked only where it is genuinely impracticable to review the entirety of the evidence and where it is clear from all the circumstances that the privilege determination will not be affected by limiting the evidence reviewed.

Subsection 4054(d)(3) requires the Government to "provide the court with a manageable index of evidence it contends is subject to the state secrets privilege," which "shall be specific enough to afford the court an adequate foundation to review the basis of the in- vocation of the privilege by the United States." This provision draws on the Vaughn indices that courts frequently require in FOIA litigation to assist their review of materials the Government claims are exempt from disclosure requirements [56]. The requirement to produce such indices will force the Government to articulate specific reasons why each item of allegedly privileged evidence contains state secrets, thus enabling "adequate adversary testing" [57] and careful judicial review of each item. As one commentator has described it, the "purpose of the detailed Vaughn Index and affidavit is to require the agency to make as full a public record as possible and to enable a more adversarial process in [a] context in which considerable asymmetry of information exists. A Vaughn Index can only serve this purpose and allow the court to perform a de novo review if it is sufficiently detailed and specific" [58]. Submission of the index to the court is not a substitute for submitting the evidence itself; rather, the purpose of the index is to serve as an interpretive aide in the court's review of the actual evidence.

Subsection 4054(e)(1) instructs the court to review each item of evidence, or each item in the sample if sampling is used under § 4052(d)(2), that the United States asserts is protected by the state secrets privilege "to determine whether the claim of the United States [that the item is privileged] is valid." "An item of evidence is subject to the state secrets privilege," the provision indicates, "if it contains a state secret, or there is no possible means of effectively segregating it from other evidence that contains a state secret." Subsection 4054(e)(2) states that non-privileged items of evidence may be publicly disclosed, subject to the standard rules of evidence and civil procedure, but that items of evidence found by the court to be privileged "shall not be disclosed or admissible as evidence." Subsection 4054(e)(3) sets a standard of judicial review for the privilege determinations made under (e)(1).

Subsection 4054(e) can be seen as the heart of the bill. It makes crystal-clear that the court, not the executive branch, determines which items of evidence are privileged. It requires the court to consider the actual evidence, rather than rely on Government affidavits or representations about the evidence, in making this determination. Following a 2005 Supreme Court ruling, it also makes clear that the privilege applies only to specific items of evidence and is therefore a strictly evidentiary privilege, distinct from the question of justiciability [59]. Finally, it sets a standard of review designed to give appropriate respect to the executive branch's institutional expertise and constitutional role, without undermining the judge's duty to make an independent determination on each privilege claim.

The requirement that the court determine for itself which items of evidence are subject to the state secrets privilege, based on its review of those items, is consistent not only with judicial review of evidentiary privilege claims generally, but also with the Supreme Court's explanation of the state secrets privilege in Reynolds (even though in Reynolds the Court ultimately declined to review the allegedly privileged evidence and therefore left itself vulnerable to being misled). The Reynolds opinion states that "[t]he court itself must determine whether the circumstances are appropriate for the claim of privilege," [60] the court must "satisfy[ ] itself that the occasion for invoking the privilege is appropriate," [61] and "judicial control over the evidence in a case cannot be abdicated to the caprice of Executive officers." 62 Subsequent judicial decisions have similarly held that a "court before which the privilege is asserted must assess the validity of the claim of privilege, satisfying itself that there is a reasonable danger that disclosure of the particular facts in litigation will jeopardize national security" [63]

All of these statements imply that the court must independently evaluate each claim of the state secrets privilege—that while the executive branch's initial privilege determination may be deserving of respect, it is never controlling, nor is it ever independent of court review. For the court to determine that the privilege applies to a particular item of evidence, it must be "ultimately satisfied that [state] secrets are at stake," [64] and there is no rational way for the court to be "ultimately satisfied" of this conclusion without looking at the evidence itself.

Reynolds thus acknowledged the authority of Federal courts to conduct in camera review of evidence that the Government claims to be privileged, when the court finds such review to be necessary. The authority of courts to review national security materials is also established in the Freedom of Information Act, which provides that courts "may examine the contents of [withheld] agency records in camera," [65] including classified records that the Government claims must be "kept secret in the interest of national defense or foreign policy." [66] To the extent that Reynolds has been read to bless the judicial practice of not "insisting upon an examination of the evidence, even by the judge alone, in chambers" under certain conditions, [67] the bill overrides the court's discretion to adopt such a practice.

In the sponsors' view, failure to scrutinize the actual evidence is an abdication of judicial responsibility, and subsection 4054(e)(1)'s requirement that the court base its privilege determinations on its own review of specific items of evidence is needed to protect against the possibility of abuse, to ensure fairness and the appearance of fairness in the use of the state secrets privilege, and to preserve the integrity of our judicial system. This requirement also recognizes and codifies the principle that state secrets assertions are jus-ticiable [68]. The justiciability of state secrets assertions was affirmed by Reynolds's statement that "[t]he court itself must determine whether the circumstances are appropriate for the claim of privilege," [69] and it has been acknowledged by numerous experts in this area of law [70].

Subsection 4054(e)(1)'s instruction that an item of evidence is subject to the privilege "if it contains a state secret, or there is no possible means of effectively segregating it from other evidence that contains a state secret," recognizes that privileged information may in some cases be inextricably entwined with non-privileged information, in which case certain otherwise non-privileged information may deserve to fall under the privilege's protection. At the same time, this provision makes clear that the court must cabin its privilege findings as tightly as it can, and that "segregation" must be used whenever possible to enforce this requirement [71]. This codifies the approach developed by the U.S. Court of Appeals for the District of Columbia Circuit, and employed by numerous courts faced with assertions of the privilege, that "whenever possible, sensitive information must be disentangled from nonsensitive information to allow for the release of the latter" [72]. If any part of an item of evidence does not contain state secrets and can be segregated from material that does contain state secrets, that part must be found non-privileged. It is the court's responsibility to determine whether such segregation is possible; it is the executive branch's responsibility to redact or delete privileged evidence as ordered.

In recent years, the executive branch has frequently asserted that seemingly harmless items of information should be protected from public disclosure, lest an adversary combine them with other items to form a dangerous mosaic [73]. While potentially useful as a heuristic for conceptualizing how adversaries utilize information, this "mosaic theory" is plainly susceptible to misuse; it lacks any limiting principle and "proves too much" by potentially covering even the most innocuous information. The requirement that judges find an item of evidence to be privileged only if the item itself "contains a state secret, or there is no possible means of effectively segregating it from other evidence that contains a state secret," is designed to prevent the Government from shielding wholly non-privileged information by invoking the mosaic theory and to warn judges against expansive applications of the theory.

Thus, to find an item of evidence to be subject to the state secrets privilege, the court must determine that public disclosure of that specific item would be reasonably likely to cause significant harm. The mosaic theory provides a metaphor for how public disclosure of evidence might be harmful; it does not alter the Government's burden of persuasion or the nature, substance, or manner of the court's review. If the Government's assertion of the privilege relies on the allegedly privileged evidence being combined with other items of information (i.e., the mosaic theory), the Government must identify specific scenarios in which the combination would be reasonably likely to cause significant harm, and it must demonstrate that such scenarios are reasonably likely to occur. The Government must show concretely and specifically, and not just through general speculation, that public disclosure of the specific items of evidence, in conjunction with other items of information, would be reasonably likely to cause significant harm.

By linking the privilege to the content of specific items of evidence and by requiring explanatory indices under subsection 4054(d)(3), the bill requires the executive branch to make precise arguments, tailored to each allegedly privileged item of evidence or portion thereof, about the consequences of disclosing the sought- after information. (Of course, the executive branch may believe that the same argument about the consequences of public disclosure obtains across multiple items of evidence; if so, it is the Government's burden to explain why.) These particularized arguments will enable the judge to evaluate the persuasiveness of the Government's state secrets assertions in a more searching and independent manner than would otherwise be possible.

Subsection 4054(e)(2) clarifies that while the state secrets privilege provides no bar to the public disclosure of non-privileged items of evidence, it provides an absolute bar to the admissibility or discoverability of privileged items. Hence, the bill not only acknowledges the necessity of withholding information in certain instances to protect national security or foreign relations; it also codifies and legitimizes the state secrets privilege. If the court determines that an item of evidence, if disclosed publicly, would be reasonably likely to cause significant harm to the national defense or foreign relations of the United States, the court may not balance this reasonable likelihood against the potential benefits that may come from public disclosure, such as revealing illegal or unconstitutional executive branch conduct, except to the extent that such benefits themselves might reduce the likelihood of "significant harm." In cases where the court determines that evidence is privileged despite certain public benefits that might result from disclosure, the court maintains its inherent authority to fashion appropriate equitable procedures or remedies that do not entail the disclosure of the privileged information As legal scholars have explained, the bill's prohibition on the release of privileged evidence undermines any constitutional objections that might possibly be raised against its basic structure:

> [A]dministration of the privilege has always been shared by the executive and the judicial branches of government. There is no constitutional bar to Congress playing an active role as well. The constitutionality of the State Secrets Protection Act is especially clear given that the Act respects and reinforces the privilege, so that if a court finds that an item of evidence contains a state secret, or cannot be effectively separated from other evidence that contains a state secret, then the evidence may not be released. Thus, even if the privilege were to have a constitutional core rooted in the President's powers under Article II of the Constitution, the Act would not encroach upon it [74].

Subsection 4054(e)(3) establishes a standard of review for courts to evaluate executive branch assertions of the state secrets privilege. In introducing this provision as an amendment at the Judiciary Committee markup, in which it passed by a vote of 18–to–1, Senator Feinstein explained that without such a provision, significant ambiguity would remain as to the intended nature of judicial review under the bill. Senator Specter, the lone dissenting vote, stated that given past executive branch abuses of the privilege, he believed the court should give no deference whatever to the executive branch's arguments as to why certain evidence deserves to be privileged. In response, Senator Feinstein emphasized that (i) "weight" is different than "deference" and is owed to all experts in litigation; (ii) some courts have been applying "utmost deference" to privilege claims, so if the bill does not address the standard of review, that standard may persist; (iii) the executive branch has a clear self-interest in lawsuits in which it is accused of breaking the law; (iv) her amendment requires the views of other relevant experts also to be given the same weight; and (v) numerous outside experts, including Judge Patricia M. Wald, have suggested "substantial weight" as the appropriate standard.

The language of subsection 4054(e)(3) reflects the belief that the executive branch's institutional expertise and constitutional responsibilities regarding national defense and foreign affairs deserve respect from the court, but that the court must make privilege determinations only on the basis of its own independent evaluation. The bill thus firmly rejects the notion that a court should give "utmost deference" to the executive branch or in any other way compromise the independence and impartiality of its decision making. This approach comports with the duty of the judiciary to safeguard constitutional rights and values and to preserve full and fair trials to the greatest extent possible (matters on which the court has far greater expertise than the executive branch), with the traditional disfavored role of evidentiary privileges in litigation, [75] and with the standard of judicial review already employed by Federal courts under FOIA's national security exemption—although the sponsors of this bill strongly reject the line of FOIA precedent that has interpreted "substantial weight" to be virtually dispositive for the Government [76].

The bill's move away from utmost deference also heeds the concern that while the executive branch may have special institutional expertise on the question of what constitutes a state secret, it is not a neutral party in lawsuits in which its agencies, officers, or contractors are being sued for allegedly illegal or unconstitutional conduct. Rather, the executive branch has an institutional self-interest in having these lawsuits dismissed—and therefore in having the state secrets privilege be construed as broadly as possible. As a result, judicial independence in the face of privilege claims is especially important [77].

To balance the testimony of a Government expert, subsection 4054(e)(3) requires the court to "weigh the testimony of a Government expert in the same manner as the court weighs, and along with, any other expert testimony in the applicable case." This language is intended not only to instruct the court on the manner of weighing Government expertise, but also to encourage greater use of non-governmental experts—again, for the fundamental reason that vigorous judicial review is needed as a check against the incentives in favor of executive branch secrecy. Non-governmental experts may be individuals who have been granted security clearances to review the allegedly privileged evidence; or, in some situations, it may be possible for individuals without clearance to provide expert assistance based on the unclassified version of the Government's affidavit required under subsection 4054(b). If no non- governmental expert is available in a given case, the court will weigh a Government expert's testimony in the same manner as it weighs expert testimony in any other case.

Importantly, subsection 4054(e)(3) rejects any notion that courts lack the competence or ability to evaluate the potential harm to national defense or foreign relations from public disclosure. Federal judges are appointed by the President, confirmed by the Senate, and take an oath to uphold the Constitution. Resolving questions of evidence and privilege are core functions of the judiciary. Numerous statutes such as CIPA, FOIA, and FISA already require courts to handle national security materials and secret information as a routine matter.78 Not once has there been any proven harm to national security, and none of these statutes has ever been seriously questioned on grounds of institutional competence. Further more, special masters and other independent advisors are available to provide technical assistance, as provided in subsection 4052(f).

Testifying before the Judiciary Committee, Judge Patricia M. Wald observed that judges "deal with national security information on a regular basis and can be entrusted with its evaluation on the relatively modest decisional threshold of whether its disclosure is 'reasonably likely' to pose a national security risk." [79]. William Webster, a former Federal judge at the district and appellate level and former head of both the FBI and CIA, stated: "I can confirm that judges can and should be trusted with sensitive information and that they are fully competent to perform an independent review of executive branch assertions of the state secrets privilege." [80].

The sponsors of this legislation agree with the statements of Judge Wald and Judge Webster. Guided by the procedures set forth in the bill, informed by its required affidavits, pre-trial hearings, and evidentiary indices, and assisted to the extent necessary by expert testimony and special masters or other independent advisors, Federal judges will have all the tools they need to make a reasoned and responsible independent evaluation of privilege claims. If the executive branch cannot persuade the court that an item of evidence is reasonably likely to cause significant harm, then that item does not deserve the extraordinary protections afforded by the state secret privilege. Moreover, the bill's provision for interlocutory appeal ensures that privileged evidence will not be disclosed on the basis of a single judge's determination, if the Government believes the determination was erroneous.

Subsection 4054(f) instructs the court, when it has found that material evidence is subject to the state secrets privilege, to order the Government, if possible, to "craft a non-privileged substitute for that privileged material evidence that provides a substantially equivalent opportunity to litigate the claim or defense as would that privileged material evidence." This role for non-privileged substitutes draws on existing practices in encouraging judges to reconcile the interests of national security with the interests of justice and the adversarial process through carefully tailored procedures, [81] and it can play a critical role in effectuating the bill's aim of minimizing the disruption to litigation caused by the privilege. While the court has the authority under this subsection to order a substitute, the executive branch is the body that would actually create the substitute, subject to the court's review.

Subsection 4054(g) states that if the court orders the Government to provide a non-privileged substitute and the Government fails to comply, the court "shall resolve the disputed issue of fact or law to which the evidence pertain in the non-government party's favor." This requirement puts teeth into the authority provided to the court in subsection 4054(f). The executive branch may refuse to turn over the substitute as ordered—which further undermines any argument that the bill unconstitutionally encroaches upon executive branch authority over alleged state secrets—but such defiance would come with an appropriately tailored penalty [82]. An analogous provision exists in CIPA, under which, if a defendant is prevented from introducing classified information needed for his or her defense, the court may dismiss the indictment or "find[] against the United States on any issue as to which the excluded classified information relates" [83].

Section 4055. In a new section 4055 of the United States Code, the bill sets forth procedures for when evidence protected by the state secrets privilege is necessary for adjudication of a claim or counterclaim.

Section 4055 allows the court to dismiss a claim or counterclaim on the basis of the state secrets privilege only if certain specified conditions are met. As indicated in subsection 4054(b), this section provides the exclusive means of dismissing a claim or counterclaim on the basis of the privilege. It is designed to reflect the sponsors' intent that, whenever possible, Federal civil cases and claims should not be dismissed—a drastic remedy strongly disfavored by constitutional and policy considerations [84] —solely on account of the state secrets privilege. Put differently, privileged evidence should never be allowed to shut down litigation that could proceed without it.

Subsection 4055(1), the first condition, indicates that a claim may not be dismissed if it is possible to produce a non-privileged substitute version of material privileged evidence that would allow the claim to be litigated fairly. Subsection 4055(2) indicates that dismissal is not allowed if it would harm national security. This provision ensures that the court will not dismiss cases in ways that would themselves jeopardize security—for example, if the very act of dismissal might tend to reveal a sensitive fact, or if the court believes that judicial resolution of an issue is needed to prevent harm to the safety and well-being of Americans. Drawing on an approach developed in recent doctrine, [85] subsection 4055(3) precludes dismissal if continuing with the litigation in the absence of the privileged evidence would not impair the ability of a party to pursue a valid defense. This provision ensures that, just as non-material privileged evidence may not be the basis for dismissal under subsection 4055(1), nor may dismissal be predicated on privileged evidence that would not be important to a party's pursuit of a valid defense.

"Valid" in subsection 4055(3) means legally and factually colorable. Thus, if the court determines through in camera review that evidence is privileged but its absence from litigation would not substantially impair the ability of a party to pursue a defense that the court determines is or may be legally and factually meritorious, then that evidence may not be the basis for dismissal on state secrets grounds. That evidence would still be excluded from the litigation on account of its privileged status, § 4054(e)(2)(A), and it could not be disclosed or admitted during trial. In some cases, the inability to use such evidence may prevent the plaintiff from making out a prime facie case, even when the evidence suggests that the plaintiff's claims may be meritorious; the bill thus accepts that in some rare and unfortunate instances, the interests of litigants may be compromised in order to protect state secrets. In other cases, however, a plaintiff may have its own evidence with which to make out a prime facie case, or may be able to make out a case with non-privileged evidence procured from the Government. In this way, the bill gives parties an opportunity to make a preliminary showing even in cases in which the privilege is found to apply [86].

These rules protect the Government and private defendants from suffering an unfair result under the bill. If a plaintiff cannot make out a case using non-privileged evidence, the defendant can, as always, prevail on summary judgment (unless the court, based on the circumstances of the case, has exercised its equitable authority to resolve relevant factual questions in the non-government party's favor). If a defendant is deprived of information needed to present a valid defense on account of the privilege, the court may dismiss the claim, thus ensuring that no party is ever put to a "Hobson's Choice" of litigating with state secrets evidence or swallowing an unwarranted adverse judgment.

In some recent cases, the Government has asserted that the "very subject matter of the action" is a state secret, such that any further proceeding would jeopardize national security [87]. To the extent that such assertions are based on the notion that the privilege may apply to a lawsuit simply because the topic of the lawsuit implicates sensitive matters, that notion is rejected. Lawsuits do not exist apart from the materials and testimony that comprise them. If the plaintiff can make out a case using only non-privileged evidence, and the defendant can present its defense using only non- privileged evidence, then clearly the case can and should proceed. To the extent that such assertions are based on the notion that the case would necessarily be "pervaded with state secrets" [88] and could not be litigated without the use of privileged evidence, the bill simply puts such categorical claims to the proof, requiring the Government to demonstrate to the court's satisfaction the extent to which state secrets pervade the lawsuit by identifying the specific items of evidence that contain state secrets. As noted above, the bill rejects the expansion of the state secrets privilege into any manner of justiciability doctrine, and demands that it be applied as a purely evidentiary privilege.

Section 4056. In a new section 4056 of the United States Code, the bill sets forth procedures for interlocutory appeal.

This section draws on CIPA [89] in allowing parties an expedited appeal of any court order under the Act, such as an order on the privileged or non-privileged status of certain items of evidence, which ensures a timely additional layer of review. This provision protects national security by ensuring that an erroneous decision by a single district court judge would not lead to the release of properly privileged evidence.

Section 4057. In a new section 4057 of the United States Code, the bill sets forth security procedures.

Subsection 4057(a) adopts security procedures established under CIPA [90] to protect against unauthorized disclosure of evidence subject to the state secrets privilege.

Subsection 4057(b) authorizes the Chief Justice of the United States, in consultation with the Attorney General, the Director of National Intelligence, and the Secretary of Defense, to create additional rules to implement the bill, subject to the review of congressional oversight committees. The Chief Justice must submit any proposed rules to appropriate congressional committees prior to their implementation. Such submission should include an explanation of why the proposed rules are needed.

All rules promulgated under this subsection must comply with the letter and the spirit of the bill, such as its goal of minimizing the disruptive effects of the state secrets privilege on civil litigation and allowing cases to be litigated to the fullest extent possible consistent with national security. The rules may include procedures to help provide for the special masters and guardians ad litem contemplated by the bill—for example, by ensuring a minimum number of guardians ad litem and special masters in each judicial district to assist parties in state secrets cases. Allowing these officials to be chosen solely by the executive branch would not "comply with the letter and spirit of the bill"; it is assumed that any rules issued on the provision of guardians ad litem and special masters will take into account the need for these officials to perform their roles without institutional bias.

Section 4058. In a new section 4058 of the United States Code, the bill provides reporting requirements.

Subsection 4058(a) requires the Attorney General to report to the House and Senate Intelligence and Judiciary Committees on each instance in which the United States claims the state secrets privilege, including providing the committees with copies of the affidavits, indices, and, upon request, the evidence. These materials shall be made available to all members of the committees. This reporting requirement enhances accountability for both the judiciary and the executive branch. By keeping Congress informed on the executive branch's use of the privilege, the reporting requirement enables Congress to formulate legislation or take other appropriate corrective action in cases in which the privilege prevents the courts from ruling on illegal or unconstitutional Government conduct or denies injured parties the relief they would otherwise be due.

Section 4058(a) thus clarifies the congressional right of access to information it needs for its legislative and oversight duties. Providing this information to Congress does not implicate the national security concerns that would attend public disclosure in litigation. The Attorney General can transmit information under "appropriate security measures," § 4058(a)(4), and Members of Congress are no less trustworthy than executive branch officials [91]. Congress has established physical security and staff clearance procedures, as well as procedures for the receipt of sensitive information, and all Members by virtue of their legislative responsibilities are entitled to classified information. As courts have recognized since the dawn of the Republic, Congress's authority to investigate executive branch activity is clearly implied in the Constitution and is a critical component of its authority to legislate and its responsibility to expose corruption and misfeasance [92]. Congressional inquiries serving legitimate interests into even the most sensitive foreign policy, military, and prosecutorial matters have consistently been upheld by the courts.

The reporting requirement established by subsection 4058(a) is intended as a floor, not a ceiling. The identification of the Intelligence and Judiciary Committees reflects the sponsors' judgment that reporting to these committees will be appropriate in all cases. However, there will undoubtedly be cases in which other committees—for example, the Armed Services and Foreign Relations Committees—should likewise be fully informed about the use of the privilege, on account of their institutional responsibilities over the implicated Government activity. It is assumed that the Intelligence and Judiciary Committees will provide access to the report and evidence transmitted under this subsection to any committee with jurisdiction over the subject matter of the lawsuit in question.

Subsection 4058(b) instructs the Attorney General to submit annual reports to the House and Senate Intelligence and Judiciary Committees on the operation and effectiveness of the legislation for three years, and afterwards as necessary. This reporting requirement supplements the requirements in subsection 4058(a) by ensuring that Congress will remain informed of the executive branch's views on the bill, as well as on its use of the privilege, and by fostering interbranch dialogue on the subject. Congress has requested recommendations and reports from the President on numerous occasions. It is the President's prerogative to decline to offer suggested amendments to the bill under subsection 4058(b), although in so doing, the President would be undermining his or her own ability to advocate any desired legislative changes.

Section 4059. In a new section 4059 of the United States Code, the bill provides a rule of construction.

This section clarifies that the bill has no effect on court judgments unrelated to, and unaffected by, the state secrets privilege, and that nothing in the bill is intended to supersede any further or additional limit on the state secrets privilege under any other provision of law. It has been argued that section 1806(f) of FISA applies to the state secrets privilege, in its instruction that the district court "shall, notwithstanding any other law, *** review in camera and ex parte [materials relating to electronic surveillance] *** to determine whether the surveillance of the aggrieved person was lawfully authorized and conducted." [93] If a court were to find that section 1806(f), or any other provision of constitutional, statutory, or judge-made law, places limits on the use or applicability of the state secrets privilege beyond the limits established under this bill, then those further or additional limits on the privilege would still apply.

SECTION 3. SEVERABILITY

This section clarifies that if any provision of the bill is held to be unconstitutional, the remainder of the bill shall not be affected thereby.

SECTION 4. APPLICATION TO PENDING CASES

This section clarifies that the bill applies to any Federal civil case pending on or after the date of its enactment.

IV. CONGRESSIONAL BUDGET OFFICE COST ESTIMATE

The Committee sets forth, with respect to the bill, S. 2533, the following estimate and comparison prepared by the Director of the Congressional Budget Office under section 402 of the Congressional Budget Act of 1974:

July 11, 2008.

Hon. PATRICK J. LEAHY,
Chairman, Committee on the Judiciary,
U.S. Senate, Washington, DC.

DEAR MR. CHAIRMAN: The Congressional Budget Office has prepared the enclosed cost estimate for S. 2533, the State Secrets Protection Act.

If you wish further details on this estimate, we will be pleased to provide them. The CBO staff contact is Leigh Angres.

Sincerely,
PETER R. ORSZAG.

Enclosure.

S. 2533—State Secrets Protection Act

CBO estimates that implementing S. 2533 would have no significant impact on the federal budget. The bill contains no intergovernmental or private-sector mandates as defined in the Unfunded Mandates Reform Act and would impose no costs on state, local, or tribal governments.

S. 2533 would codify certain practices and set limits on the federal government's use of the state secrets privilege. Under a Supreme Court ruling, the government can assert the state secrets privilege to withhold certain evidence that, if released, could harm national security. The bill would require the government to submit documents explaining the need for the privilege and allow judges to appoint experts to assess the validity of the government's claims. Finally, the bill would require the Attorney General to submit a report detailing instances when the federal government asserted the state secrets privilege.

The government has invoked the state secrets privilege 40 times in the last five years. Based on information obtained from the Department of Justice, CBO expects that the bill could alter and possibly increase litigation duties of federal attorneys. CBO estimates, however, that any resulting increase in federal spending would total less than $500,000 a year, assuming the availability of appropriated funds. Enacting S. 2533 would not affect direct spending or revenues.

The CBO staff contacts for this estimate are Leigh Angres and Jeffrey LaFave. The estimate was approved by Theresa Gullo, Deputy Assistant Director for Budget Analysis.

V. Regulatory Impact Evaluation

In compliance with rule XXVI of the Standing Rules of the Senate, the Committee finds that no significant regulatory impact will result from the enactment of S. 2533.

VI. Conclusion

By prompting the courts to apply the state secrets privilege in a clear, standardized, and rigorous way, the State Secrets Protection Act protects fundamental values, including constitutional rights, individual liberties, checks and balances, accountable Government, and access to justice. At the same time, by reinforcing the privilege and providing numerous procedural safeguards, the bill protects national security. Its systematic approach is a win-win for the rule of law and for the Nation's policy interests.

VII. Minority Views

Minority Views from Senators Hatch, Grassley, Kyl, Sessions, Graham, Cornyn, Brownback and Coburn

The protection of state secrets in civil lawsuits forces us to weigh some of our most deeply held values against one another. On one side of this issue are the important values of open government and the principle that individuals who allege that they have been wronged deserve their day in court. On the other side is the imperative that we protect national security, which often means protecting military and intelligence secrets from disclosure through the civil justice process.

Where the interests of open government and national security are in tension, it is important to strike a reasonable and workable balance between two legitimate but competing interests: the right of the people to know how their government works and the sometimes countervailing need of government to observe secrecy so that it can act effectively to protect national security, without which all the rights of the people would be in serious jeopardy.

Throughout our nation's history, two coordinate branches, the Executive and the Judiciary, have worked to strike an appropriate balance between these core values. This balance is reflected in the well-settled doctrine that courts have crafted to govern the state secrets privilege. Through a long history of constitutional and common law deliberation, the Executive and Judicial branches have struck a workable and durable compromise—one with which Congress ought not tamper without significant justification and circumspection.

Because the compromise struck by our coordinate branches of government sets the right balance between openness, justice, and national security, and because we believe that S. 2533 disrupts this balance in a way that makes it too difficult for the government to protect national security secrets, we oppose S. 2533, the "State Secrets Protection Act."

History and Content of the State Secrets Privilege

The doctrines that govern the privilege have been crafted by the Judicial Branch, and are deeply rooted in both the common law and the Constitution's separation of powers. The Common Law roots of the privilege date back at least to the early 17th Century. Edward Coke reported that a court in the early 1600s held that "concerning matters of state, which are arcana imperii [state se- crets], [1] it is met they should be kept sub sigillo concilii, and in secret." [2] By the time of the framing of the Constitution, the state secrets privilege was so enshrined in the common law that Blackstone took note of the privilege in his Commentaries on the Laws of England [3].

Cases involving whether a court may constitutionally force the Executive Branch to disclose secret information go back to the earliest days of our republic.4 In issuing a subpoena duces tecum to President Jefferson for documents relevant to the treason trial of Aaron Burr, Chief Justice John Marshall stated that "If it does contain any matter which it would be imprudent to disclose, which it is not the wish of the Executive to disclose, such matter, if it be not immediately and essentially applicable to the point, will, of course, be suppressed." [5]

The evidentiary use of the state secrets privilege in the United States has its modern roots in the Supreme Court case of United States v. Reynolds [6]. The privilege allows the government to withhold information from discovery when disclosure would be inimical to national security. The privilege is rooted in constitutional separation of powers principles as well as in the common law [7]. The privilege may be asserted by the government to resist discovery of classified information in a civil suit, and the government may intervene in a lawsuit between two private parties to prevent the production of documents that are protected by the privilege.

The privilege applies when a court is satisfied "from all the circumstances of the case, that there is a reasonable danger that compulsion of the evidence will expose military matters which, in the interest of national security, should not be divulged.''[8]. To invoke the privilege, the government must first submit a formal claim of privilege, signed by the head of the department that has control over the matter after actual personal consideration by that department head [9]. The court, not the Executive Branch, makes the ultimate determination as to whether the privilege applies [10]. In making this determination, courts give "utmost deference" to the determinations of the Executive Branch regarding the national security implications of disclosing the information [11]. The degree to which the court may "probe in satisfying itself'' that the privilege is properly invoked depends on "the showing of necessity which is made" by the party seeking production [12]. Thus, when "there is a strong showing of necessity, the claim of privilege should not be lightly accepted" [13]. However, "even the most compelling necessity cannot overcome the claim of privilege if the court is ultimately satisfied that military secrets are at stake" [14]

Reasons for Opposition to S. 2533

We oppose the bill because the existing case law strikes an appropriate balance between civil justice and national security, which the bill risks upsetting. Courts have crafted state secrets doctrine to give themselves the necessary tools to adjudicate cases and controversies that come before them, while being mindful of the Executive Branch's unique and superior expertise on matters of national security. The bill erases this constitutional and common law doctrine of the courts, and replaces it with a new and unproven scheme that risks making the protection of national security secrets too difficult.

I. The state secrets doctrine as developed by the courts strikes the right balance between the Judicial Branch's interest in doing justice and the Executive Branch's interest in protecting national security secrets

The bill is unnecessary because judges already have the necessary tools and procedures to adjudicate state secrets cases. The courts have carefully crafted state secrets doctrine to give themselves wide procedural latitude, and to preserve for themselves the ultimate determination of whether the government has proven that the state secrets privilege is properly invoked. As Senator Kennedy said in his introduction of the bill, "many of the[] powers" contained in the act "are already available to courts" under settled state secrets doctrine [15]. Because courts already have the powers they need to adjudicate these cases, legislative intervention is not urgent.

a. Because judges already have the tools and procedures that they need to adjudicate cases involving the state secrets privilege, the bill is unnecessary if not harmful

The procedural latitude that is characterized by proponents of the bill as "lack of uniformity" is a feature, not a defect, of the state secrets doctrine [16]. District judges have broad latitude in crafting the appropriate procedures for determining whether the privilege exists, and "procedural innovation" is encouraged [17]. Courts have built great flexibility into the state secrets doctrine to allow themselves the latitude to strike an appropriate balance between the rights of litigants and the needs of national security on a case-bycase basis. As the DC Circuit noted, "there is considerable variety in the situations in which a state secrets privilege may be fairly asserted. We would not wish to hobble district courts in designing procedures appropriate to novel cases" [18]

An example of the flexibility that courts have built into state secrets doctrine can be seen in the Reynolds holding that the degree to which the court may "probe in satisfying itself" that the privilege is properly invoked depends on "the showing of necessity which is made" by the party seeking production [19]. Thus, when information is very important to doing justice, courts are more skeptical of the privilege. Similarly, courts are free to take account of the level of danger posed by the particular evidence that they are considerring [20]. The interests of justice and national security are different in every case, and current doctrine gives courts the flexibility to weigh them according to each unique set of facts and circumstances.

A good example of a judge exercising this latitude can be found in Hepting v. AT&T. [21]. In that case, Judge Vaughn Walker of the Northern District of California used many of the tools contained in the bill in the process of thoroughly inspecting (and ultimately rejecting) the government's assertion of the state secrets privilege. Judge Walker ordered an in camera and ex parte review of the purportedly privileged materials, and proposed appointing an expert witness pursuant to Federal Rule of Evidence 706 to assist him in weighing the materials' national security import. Judge Walker's decision favoring the plaintiffs in Hepting was reviewed by the Ninth Circuit on an interlocutory basis. The Hepting case belies two of the key assumptions motivating the bill—that courts are unable to thoroughly review assertions of the state secrets privilege and that the government always prevails when the privilege is asserted.

The fact that courts sometimes exercise their procedural discretion to conduct a less searching review of the privilege than in cases such as Hepting does not mean that those courts are abdicating their duty to determine whether the Executive's assertion of the privilege is valid. It is central to state secrets doctrine that even after the Executive Branch has formally asserted the state secrets privilege, judges still have the ultimate authority to determine whether the evidence is covered by the privilege [22]. Executive claims of privilege are not to be lightly accepted by the courts [23].

Under the courts' state secret doctrine, in theory and in practice, the Judiciary has provided the final word.

The bill would supplant the flexibility that courts have given themselves with a rigid and mandatory regime. In doing so, it would stifle the procedural innovation that courts have said is crucial to adjudicating state secret claims in the variety of circumstances in which they arise.

b. Under the Reynolds compromise, the state secrets privilege cannot be—and has not been—lightly invoked

While current state secrets doctrine gives courts great latitude in crafting their procedures, it imposes strict rules on the Executive Branch to ensure that the privilege cannot be invoked lightly. To invoke the privilege, the Executive Branch must first submit a formal claim of privilege, signed by the head of the department that has control over the matter [24]. That department head must have actually personally considered the evidence, and determined that it is privileged [25]. After these gate-keeping formalities are met, the government still carries the burden of establishing the privilege [26].

The evidence shows that courts demand, and the government supplies, extensive evidence of the privilege's applicability before the privilege is upheld. In upholding assertions of the state secrets privilege in high-profile cases just last year, both the Ninth and Fourth Circuits described the extensively detailed evidence that the government provided in support of its privilege claim [27].

It has been said that Executive claims of the privilege rarely fail in court [28]. Perhaps this is in part because the procedural mechanism requiring a formal claim of privilege signed by a department head after personal consideration frequently accomplishes its gate- keeper role of preventing spurious assertions of the state secrets privilege [29].

Current state secrets doctrine strikes many delicate balances: between national security and the rights of litigants; between the need for rules by which a claim of privilege can be judged and the need for flexibility in responding to each case's facts and equities; and between the Executive Branch's mandate to protect national security and the Judicial Branch's mandate to uphold the law in individual cases and controversies. These balances should not be lightly discarded.

II. The bill disrupts the balance struck by the courts, and makes it too difficult for the government to protect national security secrets

Courts have developed the current state secrets doctrine through the common law process, and they retain the power to change it through that same process. The Judicial Branch has not sought to aggrandize the additional powers contained in the bill. In fact, it seems clear that courts crafted the state secrets doctrine to give deference to the Executive Branch because they were well aware of their own institutional limitations. Courts remain free to expand or contract the extent of their review under the state secrets doctrine as far as the Constitution allows. Perhaps courts could even accrue to federal judges the full powers contained in the bill. That courts have declined to aggrandize such additional powers should be powerful counsel to Congress as it considers rebalancing the courts' doctrine. Judges have consistently held that the Executive Branch is better positioned to weigh matters of national security than the Judicial Branch. Congress should not overrule the Judiciary when the Judiciary itself believes that judicial deference to executive expertise in national security matters is proper.

The bill alters the balance struck by current state secrets doctrine in several ways that could pose risks to national security. Specifically, the bill:

(a) lowers the level of deference that courts give to Executive assertions of the privilege;
(b) raises the threshold that the Executive Branch must meet to withhold state secrets;
(c) imposes impossible standards of proof against the government;
(d) makes it more difficult to protect state secrets once they have been disclosed in litigation; and
(e) makes it much more difficult for courts to dispose of meritless cases by threshold dismissal or summary judgment.

a. By lowering the standard of deference that courts give to Executive branch assertions of the privilege, the bill invites courts to substitute their judgment for that of the Executive Branch in national security matters

Under state secrets doctrine, courts give "utmost deference" to the Executive Branch's determination that materials are covered by the state secrets privilege. This "utmost deference" standard is the standard of deference most frequently adopted by courts in examining assertions of the state secrets privilege [30].

"Utmost deference" is appropriate when a court reviews the national security determinations of the Executive Branch. The Constitution gives the Executive Branch far greater power and authority over matters of national security than it gives to the Judicial Branch [31]. This constitutional separation of powers is reflected in the reality that the Executive branch department head who asserts the state secrets privilege will have national security expertise, in-telligence, and staff that dwarf that of the District Judge who reviews that assertion of the privilege [32].

Attorney General Michael Mukasey ably summarized the case law regarding the standard of deference in his March 31, 2008, letter to the Committee:

> To be sure, under current law it is the province of the Judicial branch to determine whether the state secrets privilege has been invoked properly. It is well settled, however, that the courts should make that determination by according the "utmost deference" to the expertise and judgment of national-security officials.

> E.g., Halkin v. Helms, 598 F.2d 1, 9 (D.C. Cir. 1978) ("Courts should accord the 'utmost deference' to executive assertions of privilege upon grounds of military or diplomatic secrets.") (quoting Nixon, 418 U.S. at 710). As many courts have recognized, the "utmost deference" to the judgment of the Executive branch is appropriate not only for constitutional reasons, but also for practical reasons, because national security officials "occupy a position superior to that of the courts in evaluating the consequences of a release of sensitive information." El-Masri, 479 F.3d at 305; see also Al-Haramain Islamic Foundation, Inc. v. Bush, 507 F.3d 1190, 1203 (9th Cir. 2007) ("[W]e acknowledge the need to defer to the Executive on matters of foreign policy and national security and surely cannot legitimately find ourselves second guessing the Executive in this arena."). As the courts have recognized, "[t]he significance of one item of information may frequently depend upon knowledge of many other items of information," and "[w]hat may seem trivial to the uninformed, may appear of great moment to one who has a broad view of the scene and may put the questioned item of information in its proper context." United States v. Marchetti, 466 F.2d 1309, 1318 (4th Cir. 1972). "[C]ourts are not," and should not be, "required to play with fire and chance further disclosure—inadvertent, mistaken, or even intentional—that would defeat the very purpose for which the privilege exists." Sterling v. Tenet, 416 F.3d 338, 344 (4th Cir. 2005) [33].

The bill originally contained no standard of deference. At the Committee's meeting on April 24, 2008, the Committee adopted the Feinstein Amendment to insert a "substantial weight" standard of deference into the bill. At a minimum, giving "substantial weight" to a government assertion of the privilege is significantly less than "utmost deference." But the Feinstein Amendment goes on to specify that "The court shall weigh the testimony of a government expert in the same manner as the court weighs, and along with, any other expert testimony in the applicable case." This means that a court must give the same amount of deference to the head of an Executive Branch agency testifying to protect state secrets as the court gives to an expert witness seeking their disclosure—no more, no less. Courts may not weigh the testimony of a government state secret witness more heavily, despite that he or she is an officer of a coordinate branch of government charged with protecting the national security. This is not deference at all.

By putting the Executive Branch's testimony about national security matters on the same footing as the testimony of "any other expert," the bill elevates judicial judgment above executive judgment in an area—national security—where the judicial branch is ill-equipped and ill-suited to handle such a responsibility.

Senator Kyl circulated an amendment that would have required courts to give the Executive Branch "utmost deference." The Kyl Amendment was not taken up by the Committee.

b. By raising the threshold that the government must meet to protect state secrets, the bill risks disclosure of matters which, in the interest of national security, should not be divulged

Current doctrine protects material as a state secret when "there is a reasonable danger" that disclosure "will expose military matters which, in the interest of national security, should not be divulged" [34]. The bill changes this definition to afford protection only when the evidence is "reasonably likely to cause significant harm" to national security [35]. Thus, where the government currently needs to show "a reasonable danger," under the bill the government would need to show a "reasonable likel[ihood]." Where the government currently needs to show that "in the interest of national security, [the information] should not be divulged," under the bill the government would need to show that disclosure would likely result in "significant harm." These changes would make it more difficult for the government to protect national security secrets.

The "reasonable danger" standard has been almost universally applied by courts in state secrets cases, in both cases where the government's claim of privileged prevailed, [36] and in cases where the government's claim of privilege failed [37]. By contrast, we are unaware of any case that adopts the bill's "reasonably likely to cause significant harm" standard.

The "reasonable danger" standard under current case law embodies a precautionary principle that it is best to err against exposure of national security secrets and an acknowledgement by courts that Executive officials are better positioned than judges to weigh matters of national security. This standard is consistent with the Constitution's structure. By only allowing the privilege where a court finds a likelihood of significant harm, the bill reverses the Judiciary's wisely deferential case law.

Senator Cornyn circulated an amendment that would have changed the definition of "state secret" in the bill to track the defi-nition developed by courts under current case law. The Cornyn Amendment was not taken up by the Committee.

c. The bill requires the government to meet impossible standards to protect state secrets

The bill contains several provisions that would, in effect, force the government to prove a negative. For example, if a court ruled that material was a state secret under the bill, then the government would be required to provide a non-privileged substitute for the material, unless the government could show that producing such a substitute was "impossible" [38]. This is too high a standard. Senator Brownback circulated an amendment that would have changed the word "impossible" to "not reasonably practical." The Brownback Amendment was not taken up by the Committee.

c. The bill does not do enough to protect state secrets that are disclosed in the course of litigation.

The bill would give litigants' attorneys access to evidence that the government asserts is a state secret. If the litigants' attorneys receive security clearances and participate in hearings reviewing, they will be made privy to evidence about which the state secrets privilege has been asserted. Thus, lawyers representing plaintiffs who are suing the government may gain access to information for the purposes of the hearing, even if that material is ultimately determined to be covered by the state secrets privilege. Senator Hatch's amendment to strike the provisions in the bill relating to attorney security clearances was rejected on a 10–8 party-line vote, with Senator Specter passing.

The bill would authorize disclosure of sensitive national security information to judges, court personnel, and security-cleared counsel for the limited purpose of adjudicating the state secrets claim. It is important to ensure that these participants in closed hearings under the bill do not further leak the alleged state secrets to anyone not authorized to receive the information. Senator Specter circulated amendments that would have made any disclosure of information obtained through state secret litigation under the bill a crime punishable by imprisonment. The Specter Amendments were not taken up by the Committee.

d. The bill prevents threshold dismissal of claims.

Current case law allows courts to dismiss cases based on the privilege "when the very subject of the litigation is itself a state secret," and there is "no way [the] case could be tried without compromising sensitive military secrets" [39]. Thus, while it is well-settled that "dismissal is appropriate only when no amount of effort and care on the part of the court and the parties will safeguard privileged material," it is equally well-settled that "where the very question on which a case turns is itself a state secret, or the circumstances make clear that sensitive military secrets will be so central to the subject matter of the litigation that any attempt to proceed will threaten disclosure of the privileged matters, dismissal is the appropriate remedy" [40]. The rule that a case may be dismissed when the very subject matter of the case is a state secret dates back to 1875 and Totten v. United

States, [41] in which Totten attempted to sue the United States for breach of a covert espionage contract. The Totten result makes sense—a court cannot adjudicate a contract action if the terms and existence of the contract cannot be disclosed.

The bill only allows dismissal on the basis of the state secrets privilege after court review of "all available evidence, privileged and non-privileged," and then only when (1) it is impossible to create a non-privileged substitute for privileged information, (2) dismissal would not harm national security, and (3) continuing the case without the evidence would substantially impair the ability of a party to pursue a valid defense. This would essentially eliminate the Totten doctrine, and force courts to litigate cases "the very subject of [which] is itself a state secret."

The bill actually makes a state secrets case harder to dismiss than a case that does not involve state secrets. Under the bill, a court is precluded from granting a motion to dismiss that is based even in part on the state secrets doctrine until the court has satisfied the bill's requirements, including "reviewing all available evidence." Even if the plaintiff lacks standing to bring the action, the court could be required to review all of the evidence before dismissing the case. This result wastes judicial resources and encourages abuse of process. When there are grounds for dismissal or summary judgment that are adequate and independent of any grounds related to the state secrets privilege, the court should be free to dispose of the case without conducting a wasteful hearing. Dismissal and summary judgment are important tools for disposing of meritless litigation, and courts should not be discouraged from using these tools simply because the case involves state secrets.

Conclusion

The courts are admirably loath to overturn the judgments of the Executive Branch on national security matters, because the courts recognize the Executive Branch's superior knowledge of national security. Similarly, Congress should be loath to overturn the courts' considered judgment regarding the appropriate legal standards to balance the interests of justice and national security.

The bill upsets the judicially developed balance between protection of national security and private litigants' access to secret documents. The Judiciary has crafted state secrets doctrine to give judges the flexibility to weigh these interests with appropriate deference to Executive determinations of the national interest. This judicially crafted state secrets doctrine is sufficient. S. 2533, "The

State Secrets Protection Act," is unnecessary and potentially harmful to national security

VIII. Changes to Existing Law Made by the Bill, as Reported

In compliance with paragraph 12 of rule XXVI of the Standing Rules of the Senate, changes in existing law made by S. 2533, as reported, are shown as follows (existing law proposed to be omitted is enclosed in black brackets, new matter is printed in italic, and existing law in which no change is proposed is shown in roman):

SECTION 1. SHORT TITLE

This Act may be cited as the "State Secrets Protection Act".

SEC. 2. STATE SECRETS PROTECTION

(a) IN GENERAL.—Title 28 of the United States Code is amended by adding after chapter 180, the following:

"Chapter 181—State Secrets Protection

"Sec.

"4051. Definitions.

"4052. Rules governing procedures related to this chapter.

"4053. Procedures for answering a complaint.

"4054. Procedures for determining whether evidence is protected from disclosure by the state secrets privilege.

"4055. Procedures when evidence protected by the state secrets privilege is necessary for adjudication of a claim or counterclaim.

"4056. Interlocutory appeal.

"4057. Security procedures.

"4058. Reporting.

"4059. Rule of construction.

"§4051. Definitions

"In this chapter—

"(1) the term 'evidence' means any document, witness testimony, discovery response, affidavit, object, or other material that could be admissible in court under the Federal Rules of Evidence or discoverable under the Federal Rules of Civil Procedure; and

"(2) the term 'state secret' refers to any information that, if disclosed publicly, would be reasonably likely to cause significant harm to the national defense or foreign relations of the United States.

"§4052. Rules Governing Procedures Related to This Chapter

"(a) DOCUMENTS.—A Federal court—

"(1) shall determine which filings, motions, and affidavits, or portions thereof, submitted under this chapter shall be submitted ex parte;

"(2) may order a party to provide a redacted, unclassified, or summary substitute of a filing, motion, or affidavit to other parties; and

"(3) shall make decisions under this subsection taking into consideration the interests of justice and national security

"(b) HEARINGS.—

"(1) IN CAMERA HEARINGS.—

"(A) IN GENERAL.—Except as provided in subparagraph (B), all hearings under this chapter shall be conducted in camera.

"(B) EXCEPTION.—A court may not conduct a hearing under this chapter in camera based on the assertion of the state secrets privilege if the court determines that the hearing relates only to a question of law and does not present a risk of revealing state secrets.

"(2) EX PARTE HEARINGS.—A Federal court may conduct hearings or portions thereof ex parte if the court determines, following in camera review of the evidence, that the interests of justice and national security cannot adequately be protected through the measures described in subsections (c) and (d).

"(3) RECORD OF HEARINGS.—The court shall preserve the record of all hearings conducted under this chapter for use in the event of an appeal. The court shall seal all records to the extent necessary to protect national security.

"(c) ATTORNEY SECURITY CLEARANCES.—

"(1) IN GENERAL.—A Federal court shall, at the request of the United States, limit participation in hearings conducted under this chapter, or access to motions or affidavits submitted under this chapter, to attorneys with appropriate security clearances, if the court determines that limiting participation in that manner would serve the interests of national security. The court may also appoint a guardian ad litem with the necessary security clearances to represent any party for the purposes of any hearing conducted under this chapter.

"(2) STAYS.—During the pendency of an application for security clearance by an attorney representing a party in a hearing conducted under this chapter, the court may suspend proceedings if the court determines that such a suspension would serve the interests of justice.

"(3) COURT OVERSIGHT.—If the United States fails to provide a security clearance necessary to conduct a hearing under this chapter in a reasonable period of time, the court may review in camera and ex parte the reasons of the United States for denying or delaying the clearance to ensure that the United States is not withholding a security clearance from a particular attorney or class of attorneys for any reason other than protection of national security.

(d) PROTECTIVE ORDERS.—A Federal court may issue a protective order governing any information or evidence disclosed or discussed at any hearing conducted under this chapter if the court determines that issuing such an order is necessary to protect national security.

(e) OPINIONS AND ORDERS.—Any opinions or orders issued under this chapter may be issued under seal or in redacted versions if, and to the extent that, the court determines that such measure is necessary to protect national security.

(f) SPECIAL MASTERS.—A Federal court may appoint a special master or other independent advisor who holds the necessary security clearances to assist the court in handling a matter subject to this chapter.

"§ 4053. Procedures for Answering a Complaint

(a) INTERVENTION.—The United States may intervene in any civil action in order to protect information the Government determines may be subject to the state secrets privilege.

(b) IMPERMISSIBLE AS GROUNDS FOR DISMISSAL PRIOR TO HEARINGS.—Except as provided in section 4055, the state secrets privilege shall not constitute grounds for dismissal of a case or claim. If a motion to dismiss or for summary judgment is based in whole or in part on the state secrets privilege, or may be affected by the assertion of the state secrets privilege, a ruling on that motion shall be deferred pending completion of the hearings provided under this chapter, unless the motion can be granted on grounds unrelated to, and unaffected by, the assertion of the state secrets privilege.

(c) PLEADING STATE SECRETS.—In answering a complaint, if the United States or an officer or agency of the United States is a party to the litigation, the United States may plead the state secrets privilege in response to any allegation in any individual claim or counterclaim if the admission or denial of that allegation in that individual claim or counterclaim would itself divulge a state secret to another party or the public. If the United States has intervened in a civil action, it may assert the state secrets privilege in response to any allegation in any individual claim or counterclaim if the admission or denial by a party of that allegation in that individual claim or counterclaim would itself divulge a state secret to another party or the public. No adverse inference or admission shall be drawn from a pleading of state secrets in an answer to an item in a complaint.

(d) SUPPORTING AFFIDAVIT.—In each instance in which the United States asserts the state secrets privilege in response to 1 or more claims, it shall provide the court with an affidavit signed by the head of the executive branch agency with responsibility for, and control over, the asserted state secrets explaining the factual basis for the assertion of the privilege and attesting that personal consideration was given to the assertion of the privilege. The duties of the head of an executive branch agency under this subsection may not be delegated.

"§ 4054. Procedures for Determining Whether Evidence Is Protected from Disclosure by the State Secrets Privilege

"(a) ASSERTING THE STATE SECRETS PRIVILEGE.—The United States may, in any civil action to which the United States is a party or in any other civil action before a Federal or State court, assert the state secrets privilege as a ground for withholding information or evidence in discovery or for preventing the disclosure of information through court filings or through the introduction of evidence.

"(b) SUPPORTING AFFIDAVIT.—In each instance in which the United States asserts the state secrets privilege with respect to an item of information or evidence, the United States shall provide the court with an affidavit signed by the head of the executive branch agency with responsibility for, and control over, the state secrets involved explaining the factual basis for the claim of privilege. The United States shall make public an unclassified version of the affidavit "

"(c) HEARING.—A Federal court shall conduct a hearing, consistent with the requirements of section 4052, to examine the items of evidence that the United States asserts are subject to the state secrets privilege, as well as any affidavit submitted by the United States in support of any assertion of the state secrets privilege, and to determine the validity of any assertion of the state secrets privilege made by the United States.

"(d) REVIEW OF EVIDENCE.—

"(1) SUBMISSION OF EVIDENCE.—In addition to the affidavit provided under subsection (b), and except as provided in paragraph (2) of this subsection, the United States shall make all evidence the United States claims is subject to the state secrets privilege available for the court to review, consistent with the requirements of section 4052, before any hearing conducted under this section.

"(2) SAMPLING IN CERTAIN CASES.—If the volume of evidence the United States asserts is protected by the state secrets privilege precludes a timely review of each item of evidence, or the court otherwise determines that a review of all of that evidence is not feasible, the court may substitute a sufficient sampling of the evidence if the court determines that there is no reasonable possibility that review of the additional evidence would change the determination on the privilege claim and the evidence reviewed is sufficient to enable to court to make the determination required under this section.

"(3) INDEX OF MATERIALS.—The United States shall provide the court with a manageable index of evidence it contends is subject to the state secrets privilege by formulating a system of itemizing and indexing that would correlate statements made in the affidavit provided under subsection (b) with portions of the evidence the United States asserts is subject to the state secrets privilege. The index shall be specific enough to afford the court an adequate foundation to review the basis of the invocation of the privilege by the United States.

(e) DETERMINATIONS AS TO APPLICABILITY OF STATE SECRETS PRIVILEGE.—

"(1) IN GENERAL.—Except as provided in subsection (d)(2), as to each item of evidence that the United States asserts is protected by the state secrets privilege, the court shall review, consistent with the requirements of section 4052, the specific item of evidence to determine whether the claim of the United States is valid. An item of evidence is subject to the state secrets privilege if it contains a state secret, or there is no possible means of effectively segregating it from other evidence that contains a state secret.

"(2) ADMISSIBILITY AND DISCLOSURE.—

"(A) PRIVILEGED EVIDENCE.—If the court agrees that an item of evidence is subject to the state secrets privilege, that item shall not be disclosed or admissible as evidence.

"(B) NON-PRIVILEGED EVIDENCE.—If the court determines that an item of evidence is not subject to the state secrets privilege, the state secrets privilege does not prohibit the disclosure of that item to the opposing party or the admis- sion of that item at trial, subject to the Federal Rules of Civil Procedure and the Federal Rules of Evidence.

"(3) STANDARD OF REVIEW.—The court shall give substantial weight to an assertion by the United States relating to why public disclosure of an item of evidence would be reasonably likely to cause significant harm to the national defense or foreign relations of the United States. The court shall weigh the testimony of a Government expert in the same manner as the court weighs, and along with, any other expert testimony in the applicable case.

(f) NON-PRIVILEGED SUBSTITUTE.—If the court finds that material evidence is subject to the state secrets privilege and it is possible to craft a non-privileged substitute for that privileged material evidence that provides a substantially equivalent opportunity to litigate the claim or defense as would that privileged material evidence, the court shall order the United States to provide such a substitute, which may consist of—

"(1) a summary of such privileged information;

"(2) a version of the evidence with privileged information redacted;

"(3) a statement admitting relevant facts that the privileged information would tend to prove; or

"(4) any other alternative as directed by the court in the interests of justice and protecting national security.

"(g) REFUSAL TO PROVIDE NON-PRIVILEGED SUBSTITUTE.— In a suit against the United States or an officer or agent of the United States acting in the official capacity of that officer or agent, if the court orders the United States to provide a non-privileged substitute for evidence in accordance with this section, and the United States fails to comply, the court shall resolve the disputed issue of fact or law to which the evidence pertains in the non-government party's favor.

"§ 4055. Procedures When Evidence Protected by the State Secrets Privilege Is Necessary for Adjudication of a Claim or Counterclaim

''After reviewing all pertinent evidence, privileged and non-privileged, a Federal court may dismiss a claim or counterclaim on the basis of the state secrets privilege only if the court determines that—

(a) it is impossible to create for privileged material evidence a non-privileged substitute under section 4054(f) that provides a substantially equivalent opportunity to litigate the claim or counterclaim as would that privileged material evidence;

(b) dismissal of the claim or counterclaim would not harm national security; and

(c) continuing with litigation of the claim or counterclaim in the absence of the privileged material evidence would substantially impair the ability of a party to pursue a valid defense to the claim or counterclaim.

“§ 4056. Interlocutory Appeal

"(a) IN GENERAL.—The courts of appeal shall have jurisdiction of an appeal by any party from any interlocutory decision or order of a district court of the United States under this chapter.

"(b) APPEAL.—

"(1) IN GENERAL.—An appeal taken under this section either before or during trial shall be expedited by the court of appeals.

"(2) DURING TRIAL.—If an appeal is taken during trial, the district court shall adjourn the trial until the appeal is resolved and the court of appeals—

"(a) shall hear argument on appeal as expeditiously as possible after adjournment of the trial by the district court;

"(b) may dispense with written briefs other than the supporting materials previously submitted to the trial court;

"(c) shall render its decision as expeditiously as possible after argument on appeal; and

"(d) may dispense with the issuance of a written opinion in rendering its decision.

“§ 4057. Security Procedures

"(a) IN GENERAL.—The security procedures established under the Classified Information Procedures Act (18 U.S.C. App.) by the Chief Justice of the United States for the protection of classified information shall be used to protect against unauthorized disclosure of evidence protected by the state secrets privilege.

"(b) RULES.—The Chief Justice of the United States, in consultation with the Attorney General, the Director of National Intelligence, and the Secretary of Defense, may create additional rules or amend the rules to implement this chapter and shall submit any such additional rules or amendments to the Permanent Select Committee on Intelligence and the Committee on the Judiciary of the House of Representatives and the Select Committee on Intelligence and the Committee on the Judiciary of the Senate. Any such rules or amendments shall become effective 90 days after such submission, unless Congress provides otherwise. Rules and amendments shall comply with the letter and spirit of this chapter, and may include procedures concerning the role of magistrate judges and special masters in assisting courts in carrying out this chapter. The rules or amendments under this subsection may include procedures to ensure that a sufficient number of attorneys with appropriate security clearances are available in each of the judicial districts of the United States to serve as guardians ad litem under section 4052 (c) (1).

"§ 4058. Reporting

"(a) ASSERTION OF STATE SECRETS PRIVILEGE.—

"(1) IN GENERAL.—The Attorney General shall submit to the Permanent Select Committee on Intelligence and the Committee on the Judiciary of the House of Representatives and the Select Committee on Intelligence and the Committee on the Judiciary of the Senate a report on any case in which the United States asserts the state secrets privilege, not later than 30 calendar days after the date of such assertion.

"(2) CONTENTS.—Each report submitted under this subsection shall include any affidavit filed in support of the assertion of the state secrets privilege and the index required under section 4054(d)(2).

"(3) EVIDENCE.—Upon a request by any member of the Permanent Select Committee on Intelligence or the Committee on the Judiciary of the House of Representatives or the Select Committee on Intelligence or the Committee on the Judiciary of the Senate, the Attorney General shall provide to that member any item of evidence relating to which the United States has asserted the state secrets privilege.

"(4) PROTECTION OF INFORMATION.—An affidavit, index, or item of evidence provided under this subsection may be included in a classified annex or provided under any other appropriate security measures.

"(b) OPERATION AND EFFECTIVENESS.—

"(1) IN GENERAL.—The Attorney General shall deliver to the committees of Congress described in subsection (a) a report concerning the operation and effectiveness of this chapter and including suggested amendments to this chapter.

"(2) DEADLINE.—The Attorney General shall submit a report under paragraph (1) not later than 1 year after the date of enactment of this chapter, and every year thereafter until the date that is 3 years after that date of enactment. After the date that is 3 years after that date of enactment, the Attorney General shall submit a report under paragraph (1) as necessary.

"§ 4059. Rule of Construction

"Nothing in this chapter—

"(1) is intended to supersede any further or additional limit on the state secrets privilege under any other provision of law; or

"(2) may be construed to preclude a court from dismissing a claim or counterclaim or entering judgment on grounds unrelated to, and unaffected by, the assertion of the state secrets privilege.".

(b) TECHNICAL AND CONFORMING AMENDMENT.—The table of chapters for title 28, United States Code, is amended by adding at the end the following:

"181. State secrets protection 4051"

SEC. 3. SEVERABILITY

If any provision of this Act, any amendment made by the Act, or the application of such provision or amendment to any person or circumstances is held to be invalid, the remainder of this Act, the amendments made by the Act, and the application of such provisions to persons or circumstances other than those to which it is held invalid, shall not be affected thereby.

SEC. 4. APPLICATION TO PENDING CASES

The amendments made by this Act shall apply to any civil case pending on or after the date of enactment of this Act.

REFERENCES

[1] See Louis Fisher, In the Name of National Security: Unchecked Presidential Power and the Reynolds Case 141–44 (2006); Robert M. Chesney, State Secrets and the Limits of National Security Litigation, 75 Geo. Wash. L. Rev. 1249, 1292 (2007).

[2] 345 U.S. 1 (1953).

[3] See, e.g., Louis Fisher, In the Name of National Security: Unchecked Presidential Power and the Reynolds Case (2006); Neil Kinkopf, The State Secrets Problem: Can Congress Fix It?, 80 Temp. L. Rev. 489, 492–93 (2007); William G. Weaver & Danielle Escontrias, Origins of the State Secrets Privilege 57–66 (Feb. 10, 2008) (unpublished manuscript), available at http://papers.ssrn.com/abstract=1079364; Justin Florence & Matthew Gerke, State Your Secrets: The Smart Way Around Telecom Immunity, Slate, Nov. 14, 2007, http://www.slate.com/id/2177962.

[4] See, e.g., Louis Fisher, Congressional Access to National Security Information, 45 Harv. J. on Legis. 219, 220 (2008) ("Federal courts vary widely in interpreting their duties when the Executive Branch claims [the state secrets] privilege. Some courts insist that the trial judge should receive the disputed documents and examine them in camera. Others adopt judicial standards ranging from 'deference' to 'utmost deference' to treating the privilege as an 'absolute.''' (internal citations omitted)); Carrie Newton Lyons, The State Secrets Privilege: Expanding Its Scope Through Government Misuse, 11 Lewis & Clark L. Rev. 99, 132 (2007) (describing "deviations from Reynolds'' that are "interfering with the opportunity to pursue claims of violations of private and public constitutional rights''); John Cary Sims, Ten Questions: Responses of John Cary Sims, 33 Wm. Mitchell L. Rev. 1593, 1597 (2007) ("Have the executive branch's recent assertions of the state secrets privilege broken from the doctrinal moorings of the Reynolds decision? Yes. * * * [T]he state secrets doctrine has been expanded beyond all reason * * *.'').

[5] Robert M. Chesney, State Secrets and the Limits of National Security Litigation, 75 Geo. Wash. L. Rev. 1249, 1251–52 (2007).

[6] See William G. Weaver & Robert M. Pallitto, State Secrets and Executive Power, 120 Pol. Sci. Q. 85, 101 (2005) ("Use of the state secrets privilege in courts has grown significantly over the last twenty-five years. In the twenty-three years between the decision in Reynolds and the election of Jimmy Carter, in 1976, there were four reported cases in which the Government invoked the privilege. Between 1977 and 2001, there were a total of fifty-one

reported cases in which courts ruled on invocation of the privilege."); Scott Shane, Invoking Secrets Privilege Becomes a More Popular Legal Tactic by U.S., N.Y. Times, June 4, 2006, at A32 (describing recent cases); Scholars' Letter to Senate Judiciary Committee 1 (Feb. 12, 2008) ("Although the privilege was asserted sparingly over the first few decades of its existence, it has been raised with increasing frequency over the past twenty years by both Democratic and Republican administrations. The privilege has been cited not only as grounds for withholding evidence, but also as a basis for the immediate dismissal, prior to discovery, of entire categories of cases challenging the legality of executive conduct.").

[7] See, e.g., Am. Civil Liberties Union v. Nat'l Sec. Agency, 493 F.3d 644 (6th Cir. 2007), cert. denied, 128 S. Ct. 1334 (2008); Al-Haramain Islamic Found., Inc. v. Bush, 507 F.3d 1190 (9th Cir. 2007); Terkel v. AT&T Corp., 441 F. Supp. 2d 899 (N.D. Ill. 2006); Hepting v. AT&T Corp., 439 F. Supp. 2d 974 (N.D. Cal. 2006).

[8] See, e.g., Sterling v. Tenet, 416 F.3d 338 (4th Cir. 2005), cert. denied sub nom Sterling v. Goss, 546 U.S. 1093 (2006).

[9] See, e.g., Edmonds v. U.S. Dep't of Justice, 323 F. Supp. 2d 65 (D.D.C. 2004).

[10] See, e.g., El-Masri v. Tenet, 437 F. Supp. 2d 530 (E.D. Va. 2006), aff'd 479 F.3d 296 (4th Cir. 2007), cert. denied, 128 S. Ct. 373 (2007); Arar v. Ashcroft, 414 F. Supp. 2d 250 (E.D.N.Y. 2006); Mohamed v. Jeppesen Dataplan, Inc., 539 F. Supp. 2d 1128 (N.D. Cal. 2008).

[11] Amanda Frost, The State Secrets Privilege and Separation of Powers, 75 Fordham L. Rev. 1931, 1950 (2007). Professor Robert Chesney has argued that "that the Bush administration does not differ qualitatively from its predecessors in its use of the privilege, which since the early 1970s has frequently been the occasion for abrupt dismissal of lawsuits alleging government misconduct." Robert M. Chesney, State Secrets and the Limits of National Security Litigation, 75 Geo. Wash. L. Rev. 1249, 1249 (2007); see also id. ("I also conclude that the quantitative inquiry serves little purpose in light of variation in the number of occasions for potential invocation of the privilege from year to year."). Other scholars dispute this contention. See, e.g., Frost, supra, at 1939–40 ("T]he Bush Administration's recent assertion of the privilege differs from past practice in that it is seeking blanket dismissal of every case challenging the constitutionality of specific, ongoing government programs. In comparison, the government responded to lawsuits brought in the 1970s and 1980s challenging its warrantless surveillance programs by seeking to limit discovery, and only

rarely filed motions to dismiss the entire litigation. The current practice is thus unique." (internal citation omitted)); Meredith Fuchs, Judging Secrets: The Role Courts Should Play in Preventing Unnecessary Secrecy, 58 Admin. L. Rev. 131, 134 (2006) ("In the courts, the government has dramatically increased use of potent litigation tactics such as motions to dismiss lawsuits on the basis of state secrets privilege."); John Cary Sims, Ten Questions: Responses of John Cary Sims, 33 Wm. Mitchell L. Rev. 1593, 1598 (2007) ("The state secrets doctrine is quickly becoming an additional and almost-impermeable immunity doctrine * * *."); William G. Weaver & Robert M. Pallitto, State Secrets and Executive Power, 120 Pol. Sci. Q. 85, 109 (2005) ("[R]ecent cases indicate that Bush administration lawyers are using the privilege with offhanded abandon."); see also Letter from William G. Weaver, Associate Professor, University of Texas at El Paso, and Danielle Escontrias to Senator Kennedy (Feb. 8, 2008) (disputing Professor Chesney's methodology and conclusions)

[12] Robert M. Chesney, State Secrets and the Limits of National Security Litigation, 75 Geo. Wash. L. Rev. 1249, 1267 n.113 (2007) (providing numerous citations).

[13] See Michael H. Page, Note, Judging Without the Facts: A Schematic for Reviewing State Secrets Privilege Claims, 93 Cornell L. Rev. (forthcoming 2008) (noting that "[c]ommentators have almost universally criticized the state secrets privilege" and that "[m]any commentators have criticized the courts for being overly deferential to the government's claims of privilege" and providing citations). Examples of recent critiques include Louis Fisher, In the Name of National Security: Unchecked Presidential Power and the Reynolds Case chs. 7–8 (2006); Timothy Casey, Electronic Surveillance and the Right To Be Secure, 41 U.C. Davis L. Rev. 977, 1024– 25 (2008); Amanda Frost, The State Secrets Privilege and Separation of Powers, 75 Fordham L. Rev. 1931 (2007); Lisa Graves, Ten Questions: Responses of Lisa Graves, 33 Wm. Mitchell L. Rev. 1619, 1622–23 (2007); Neil Kinkopf, The State Secrets Problem: Can Congress Fix It?, 80 Temp. L. Rev. 489 (2007); Carrie Newton Lyons, The State Secrets Privilege: Expanding Its Scope Through Government Misuse, 11 Lewis & Clark L. Rev. 99 (2007); John Cary Sims, Ten Questions: Responses of John Cary Sims, 33 Wm. Mitchell L. Rev. 1593, 1597–99 (2007); D.A. Jeremy Telman, Our Very Privileged Executive: Why the Judiciary Can (and Should) Fix the State Secrets Privilege, 80 Temp. L. Rev. 499 (2007); David C. Vladeck, Litigating National Security Cases in the Aftermath of 9/11, 2 J. Nat'l Security L. & Pol'y 165, 186–92 (2006); William G. Weaver & Robert M.

Pallitto, State Secrets and Executive Power, 120 Pol. Sci. Q. 85 (2005); Robyn Blumner, Injustice Hides Behind Badge of Security, St. Petersburg Times, Feb. 10, 2008, at 5P; Susan Burgess, Cases Without Courts, News Media & L., July 1, 2006, at 32; Editorial, Privileged Tyranny, Daytona News-J., Mar. 13, 2008, at A4; Editorial, Secrets and Rights, N.Y. Times, Feb. 2, 2008, at A18; Editorial, Secure Lawsuits, Wash. Post, Mar. 6, 2008, at A20; Editorial, What's a Secret?, Wash. Post, Apr. 11, 2008, at A20; Editorial, Whose Privilege?, N.Y. Times, Apr. 18, 2008, at A24; Bruce Fein, State Secrets Abuse, Wash. Times, Mar. 13, 2007, at A16; Justin Florence & Matthew Gerke, State Your Secrets, Slate, Nov. 14, 2007, http:// www.slate.com/id/2177962; Henry Lanman, Secret Guarding, Slate, May 22, 2006, http:// www.slate.com/id/2142155; Ben Wizner, Shielded by Secrecy, L.A. Times, Feb. 14, 2008, at A25.

[14] 18 U.S.C. app. 3 §§ 1–16 (2000).

[15] 5 U.S.C. §552 (2000).

[16] 50 U.S.C. §§ 1801–1811 (2000).

[17] See supra note 4 and accompanying text; see also William G. Weaver & Danielle Escontrias, Origins of the State Secrets Privilege 68 (Feb. 10, 2008) (unpublished manuscript), available at http://papers.ssrn.com/ abstract=1079364 ("[T]he decision in Reynolds is devoid of policy, theory, or principles to guide lower courts.").

[18] See Am. Civil Liberties Union v. Nat'l Sec. Agency, 493 F.3d 644 (6th Cir. 2007), cert. denied, 128 S. Ct. 1334 (2008); El-Masri v. Tenet, 479 F.3d 296 (4th Cir. 2007), cert. denied, 128 S. Ct. 373 (2007).

[19] Scholars' Letter to Senate Judiciary Committee 2 (Feb. 12, 2008); see also Examining the State Secrets Privilege: Protecting National Security While Preserving Accountability, Hearing before the S. Comm. on the Judiciary, 110th Cong. (Feb. 13, 2008) (statement of Patricia M. Wald) (explaining that "there has not been uniformity in the case law surrounding what the judges should do in administering the privilege" and stating that it would "be helpful to [judges] to have a protocol, to have a series of steps they must go forward with * * * [to] produce more uniform results"); Examining the State Secrets Privilege: Protecting National Security While Preserving Accountability, Hearing before the S. Comm. on the Judiciary, 110th Cong. (Feb. 13, 2008) (prepared statement of H. Thomas Wells, Jr., President-Elect, American Bar Association) ("Courts have been required to evaluate [claims of the state secrets] privilege without the benefit of statutory guidance or clear precedent. This has resulted in the application of inconsistent standards and procedures in determinations regarding the

applicability of the privilege."); Letter from Michael W. Macleod-Ball & Michael German, Am. Civil Liberties Union, to Senators Patrick Leahy and Arlen Specter 3 (Apr. 2, 2008) (lamenting the "substantial confusion in the lower courts regarding both when the privilege properly may be invoked, and what precisely the privilege may be invoked to protect," as well as regarding "how deeply a court must probe the government's claim of the privilege, and what, exactly, the court must examine in assessing a privilege claim").

[20] The controversial El-Masri decision, for example, featured each of these practices. See ElMasri v. Tenet, 437 F. Supp. 2d 530 (E.D. Va. 2006), aff'd 479 F.3d 296 (4th Cir. 2007), cert. denied, 128 S. Ct. 373 (2007); see also Editorial, Supreme Disgrace, N.Y. Times, Oct. 11, 2007, at A30 (excoriating the Supreme Court for denying Mr. El-Masri's petition for certiorari and observing that the state secrets privilege "was originally intended to shield specific evidence in a lawsuit filed against the government" and "was never designed to dictate dismissal of an entire case before any evidence is produced").

[21] William G. Weaver & Robert M. Pallitto, State Secrets and Executive Power, 120 Pol. Sci. Q. 85, 101 (2005).

[22] Id. (quoting United States v. Reynolds, 345 U.S. 1, 9–10 (1953)); see also William G. Weaver & Danielle Escontrias, Origins of the State Secrets Privilege 65–66 (Feb. 10, 2008) (unpublished manuscript), available at http://papers.ssrn.com/abstract=1079364 ("It is difficult to conclude other than that courts have simply abandoned the field of a contentious area of law.").

[23] 345 U.S. 1 (1953).

[24] See Louis Fisher, In the Name of National Security: Unchecked Presidential Power and the Reynolds Case (2006).

[25] Examining the State Secrets Privilege: Protecting National Security While Preserving Accountability, Hearing before the S. Comm. on the Judiciary, 110th Cong. (Feb. 13, 2008) (prepared statement of Louis Fisher). The decedents' families recently tried to have their lawsuit reopened on the basis of fraud on the court, but their petition was denied on account of the high bar to overcoming judicial finality. Herring v. United States, 2004 WL 2040272 (E.D. Pa. Sept. 10, 2004), aff'd 424 F.3d 384 (3d Cir. 2005), cert. denied 547 U.S. 1123 (2006).

[26] Patrick Radden Keefe, State Secrets: A Government Misstep in a Wiretapping Case, New Yorker, Apr. 28, 2008, at 28; see also Report of the Commission on Protecting and Reducing Government Secrecy, S. Doc. No.

105–2, at 8 (1997) ("As the scope of secrecy grows * * *, the prospect for leaks—deliberate releases of classified information, nearly always on an anonymous basis—grows as well. Secrets become vulnerable to betrayal, often from high in the chain of command; this in turn promotes greater disrespect for the system itself.").

[27] Am. Bar Ass'n, Report to the House of Delegates 1 (Revised Report 116A) (2007).

[28] Constitution Project, Reforming the State Secrets Privilege, at ii (2007).

[29] Scholars' Letter to Members of Congress 3–4 (Oct. 4, 2007).

[30] Examining the State Secrets Privilege: Protecting National Security While Preserving Accountability, Hearing before the S. Comm. on the Judiciary, 110th Cong. (Feb. 13, 2008) (prepared statement of Patricia M. Wald).

[31] See, e.g., In re United States, 872 F.2d 472, 474 (D.C. Cir. 1989) ("[T]he exact origins of the privilege are not certain * * *."); Robert M. Chesney, State Secrets and the Limits of National Security Litigation, 75 Geo. Wash. L. Rev. 1249, 1270–1308 (2007) (tracing the history of the privilege); William G. Weaver & Danielle Escontrias, Origins of the State Secrets Privilege (Feb. 10, 2008) (unpublished manuscript), available at http://papers.ssrn.com/ abstract=1079364 (locating the origins of the privilege in English crown prerogative).

[32] Compare United States v. Reynolds, 345 U.S. 1, 6 (1953) (stating that preclusive Executive Branch assertions of the privilege have "constitutional overtones which we find it unnecessary to pass upon"); and Robert M. Chesney, State Secrets and the Limits of National Security Litigation, 75 Geo. Wash. L. Rev. 1249, 1309–10 (2007) (suggesting that the privilege has a "constitutional core surrounded by a revisable common-law shell"); with Reynolds, 345 U.S. at 6– 7 (describing the privilege as "well established in the law of evidence" (emphasis added)); Mon-arch Assur. P.L.C. v. United States, 244 F.3d 1356, 1358 (Fed. Cir. 2001) (describing the "com- mon-law state secrets privilege"); kasza v. Browner, 133 F.3d 1159, 1165 (9th Cir. 1998) (describing the privilege as "a common law evidentiary privilege that allows the government to deny discovery of military secrets"); In re United States, 872 F.2d 472, 474 (D.C. Cir. 1989) (describing the privilege as "a common law evidentiary rule"); and Fed R. Evid. 501 notes of Committee on the Judiciary, H. Rep. No. 93–650 (describing the "secrets of state" privilege as one of nine "nonconstitutional privileges" that the Supreme Court submitted to Congress). In United States v. Nixon, 418 U.S. 683, 708 (1974), the Supreme Court stated that the presidential communications privilege is "inextricably rooted in the separation of powers

under the Constitution," but the Court has never made any comparable pronouncement on the state secrets privilege.

[33] See, e.g., Am. Bar Ass'n, Report to the House of Delegates 1 (Revised Report 116A) (2007) (analogizing to the Classified Information Procedures Act in urging Congress to enact legislation on the privilege); Constitution Project, Reforming the State Secrets Privilege 14 (2007) (asserting that "our constitutional system of checks and balances" will be jeopardized unless Congress enacts legislation on the privilege); Amanda Frost, The State Secrets Privilege and Separation of Powers, 75 Fordham L. Rev. 1931, 1932–33, 1951–56 (2007) (stating that, in this area as in others, "Congress's power to confer jurisdiction permits Congress to work together with courts to police the activities of the executive branch"); Neil Kinkopf, The State Secrets Problem: Can Congress Fix It?, 80 Temp. L. Rev. 489, 494–98 (2007) (cataloguing constitutional "powers [that] provide a strong basis for Congress to respond to the growing problems raised by the state secrets privilege"); Examining the State Secrets Privilege: Protecting National Security While Preserving Accountability, Hearing before the S. Comm. on the Judiciary, 110th Cong. (Feb. 13, 2008) (statement of Louis Fisher) ("Congress has all the legitimacy in the world to provide the guidelines [on judicial review of the privilege]."); id. (statement of Robert Chesney) ("The power to regulate, I think it's clearly within the constitutional power of Congress to create rules that will govern the process of the privilege, and so on and so forth."); Letter from Aziz Huq and Emily Berman, Brennan Center for Justice, to David Pozen 2–4 (Apr. 3, 2008) (explaining why, even assuming arguendo that the privilege is constitutionally based, "state secrets legislation would not trench on Article II authority"). Cf. Herbert v. Lando, 441 U.S. 153, 175 (1979) ("Evidentiary privileges in litigation are not favored, and even those rooted in the Constitution must give way in proper circumstances." (citing United States v. Nixon, 418 U.S. 683 (1974)); Youngstown Sheet & Tube Co. v. Sawyer, 343 U.S. 579, 637 (1952) (Jackson, J., concurring) (observing that, in matters of national security as in all others, the President's power to pursue a course of action is diminished to the extent that Congress regulates that action pursuant to its constitutional authorities).

[34] U.S. Const. art. III, §2, cl. 2 (expressly granting Congress the power to enact "Regulations" concerning the jurisdiction of Federal courts); see also Dickerson v. United States, 530 U.S. 428, 437 (2000) ("Congress retains the ultimate authority to modify or set aside any judicially created rules of evidence and procedure that are not required by the Constitution."); Sibbach

v. Wilson & Co., 312 U.S. 1, 9–10 (1941) ("Congress has undoubted power to regulate the practice and procedure of federal courts * * *.").

[35] See Hamdan v. Rumsfeld, 126 S. Ct. 2749, 2773–74 (2006) (discussing the enumerated powers granted to Congress in a time of war); Hamdi v. Rumsfeld, 542 U.S. 507, 582 (2004) (Thomas, J., dissenting) (noting Congress's "substantial and essential role in both foreign affairs and national security"); Afroyim v. Rusk, 387 U.S. 253, 256 (1967) (reaffirming that "Congress has an implied power to deal with foreign affairs as an indispensable attribute of sovereignty"); Aptheker v. Sec'y of State, 378 U.S. 500, 509 (1964) ("That Congress under the Constitution has power to safeguard our Nation's security is obvious and unarguable."); Letter from 23 Constitutional Law Scholars to Congress at 2, 6, available at http://www.law.duke.edu/features/pdf/congresslpowerlletter.pdf (cataloguing the "extensive powers relating to war" explicitly granted by the Constitution to Congress and explaining the Supreme Court's consistent reliance on Justice Jackson's concurrence in Youngstown Sheet & Tube Co. v. Sawyer to require the President to comply with applicable statutory limits in wartime); see also Hamdi, supra, 542 U.S. at 536 ("Whatever power the United States Constitution envisions for the Executive in its exchanges with other nations or with enemy organizations in times of conflict, it most assuredly envisions a role for all three branches when individual liberties are at stake.").

[36] U.S. Const. art. I, §8, cl. 18.

[37] This Administration and recent predecessors have relied heavily on Department of Navy v. Egan, 484 U.S. 518 (1988), for the proposition that statutes regulating the disclosure of sensitive national security information may raise constitutional concerns. See David J. Barron & Martin S. Lederman, The Commander in Chief at the Lowest Ebb—A Constitutional History, 121 Harv. L. Rev. 941, 1084–85 (2008) (providing recent examples). However, the Supreme Court's statement in Egan that "unless Congress specifically has provided otherwise, courts traditionally have been reluctant to intrude upon the authority of the Executive in military and national security affairs," 484 U.S. at 530 (emphasis added), plainly implies that Congress possesses the constitutional authority to pass such regulations. It is also instructive to note that the Court in Egan appears to have adopted this formulation from the Justice Department itself, which argued in its brief that "[a]bsent an unambiguous grant of jurisdiction by Congress, courts have traditionally been reluctant to intrude upon the authority of the executive in military and national security affairs." Brief for the Petitioner at 21, Egan, 484 U.S. 518 (1988) (No. 86–1552) (emphasis added).

[38] In July 21, 2008, remarks to the American Enterprise Institute, Attorney General Michael Mukasey endorsed legislative intervention in cases implicating national security when there exists a "serious risk of inconsistent rulings and considerable uncertainty," and noted that congressional action to provide procedures in national security cases is "well within the historic role and competence of Congress." Att'y Gen. Michael B. Mukasey, Speech at the American Enterprise Institute for Public Policy Research (July 21, 2008), available at http://www.usdoj.gov/ ag / speeches / 2008 / ag-speech-0807213.html. Although he was proposing action in another setting, the Attorney General's arguments likewise support legislation to standardize and clarify the procedures governing the state secrets privilege.

[39] 154 Cong. Rec. S198 (daily ed. Jan. 23, 2008) (statement of Sen. Kennedy).

[40] 154 Cong. Rec. S199 (daily ed. Jan. 23, 2008) (statement of Sen. Specter)

[41] Statement of Senator Patrick Leahy (Feb 13, 2008), http://leahy.senate.gov/press/200802/021308a.html.

[42] Letter from Senator Kennedy, Senator Leahy and Senator Specter to Senate Colleagues (Feb. 25, 2008).

[43] The following materials were submitted for the record: April 2, 2008 letter from Louis Fisher (Library of Congress) to Senator Kennedy; April 2, 2008 letter from Kevin S. Bankston (Electronic Frontier Foundation), Jon P. Eisenberg (Eisenberg & Hancock LLP), Caroline Fredrickson (American Civil Liberties Union), and Gregory T. Nojeim (Center for Democracy & Technology) to Senators Leahy and Specter; April 2, 2008 letter from Sharon Bradford Franklin and Virginia E. Sloan (Constitution Project) to Senators Leahy and Specter; April 2, 2008 letter from Michael W. Macleod-Ball and Michael German (American Civil Liberties Union) to Senators Leahy and Specter; April 2, 2008 letter from Denise A. Cardman (American Bar Association) to Senators Leahy and Specter; April 3, 2008 letter from Aziz Huq and Emily Berman (Brennan Center for Justice) to David Pozen; February 12, 2008 letter to the Senate Committee on the Judiciary by 11 scholars of constitutional law and national security; April 28, 2008 editorial, Whose Privilege?, by the New York Times; February 2, 2008 editorial, Secrets and Rights, by the New York Times; April 11, 2008 editorial, What's a Secret?, by the Washington Post; and March 6, 2008 editorial, Secure Lawsuits, by the Washington Post.

[44] In this regard, it is worth noting that there is a longstanding bipartisan "consensus that the executive habitually overclassifies" documents, Adam M. Samaha, Government Secrets, Constitutional Law, and Platforms for

Judicial Intervention, 53 UCLA L. Rev. 909, 940 (2006), and that recent U.S. history contains numerous examples of executive branch claims of secrecy that turned out to be greatly exaggerated. See, e.g., Erwin N. Griswold, Secrets Not Worth Keeping, Wash. Post, Feb. 15, 1989, at A25 (stating that ''[i]t quickly becomes apparent to any person who has considerable experience with classified material that there is massive overclassification and that the principle concern of the classifiers is not with national security, but rather with governmental embarrassment of one sort or another,'' and acknowledging that he had "never seen any trace of a threat to the national security'' in the landmark Pentagon Papers case that he litigated as Solicitor General); see also Report of the Commission on Protecting and Reducing Government Secrecy: Hearing Before the Comm. on Governmental Affairs, 105th Cong. app. at 23 (1997) ("It is no secret that the government classifies too much information.'') (statement of J. William Leonard, Director, Information Security Oversight Office, National Archives and Records Administration); Donald Rumsfeld, War of the Worlds, Wall St. J., July 18, 2005, at A12 ("I have long believed that too much material is classified across the federal government as a general rule***'').

[45] 345 U.S. 1, 10 (1953).

[46] See, e.g., In re Sealed Case, 494 F.3d 139, 142 (D.C. Cir. 2007); In re United States, 872 F.2d 472, 474 (D.C. Cir. 1989).

[47] See, e.g., Zuckerbraun v. General Dynamics Corp., 935 F.2d 544, 546–47 (2d Cir. 1991).

[48] See, e.g., Ellsberg v. Mitchell, 709 F.2d 51, 56 (D.C. Cir. 1983).

[49] Robert M. Chesney accurately captured the intent of the legislation's sponsors to clarify the definition of "state secret'' in civil litigation, rather than fundamentally to transform the definition. In response to written questions from Judiciary Committee Members about how the bill's definition of "state secret'' compares to current law, Professor Chesney stated: "It seems to me that there are two variables at issue here. First there is the question of how likely it is that public disclosure of information will cause harm, period. Second, there is the question of the magnitude of that harm. The language in the bill calibrates the first variable using a reasonable-risk test that is, I think, consistent with existing law (as reflected in the "reasonable danger'' language quoted above). The language in the bill calibrates the second variable using a "significant harm'' standard. How does that compare to the status quo? I do not think there is a clear answer to that question. Reynolds and its progeny do not clearly specify whether the

harm threshold is de minimis, significant, grave, or any other particular calibration. That said, it seems to me that "significant" fairly captures the understanding implicit in current law, given that there is no affirmative support in current law for the proposition that the privilege only kicks in when the harm to national security would be especially grave, and given that there is little sense in protecting information the disclosure of which concededly would cause only de minimis or insignificant harms. For all of those reasons, therefore, I think that the bill does not actually work a change with respect to either variable."—Response of Robert M. Chesney to Written Questions 4–5 (Mar. 5, 2008).

[50] See, e.g., El-Masri v. United States, 479 F.3d 296, 305 (4th Cir. 2007); In re Grand Jury Subpoena dated August 9, 2000, 218 F. Supp. 2d 544, 559 (S.D.N.Y. 2002).

[51] Cf. Kerr v. U.S. Dist. Court, 426 U.S. 394, 405–06 (1976) ("It is settled that in camera procedures are an appropriate means to resolve disputed issues of privilege."); Mark J. Rozell, Executive Privilege: Presidential Power, Secrecy, and Accountability 165 (rev. 2d ed. 2002) ("There * * * is considerable legal precedent for in camera review of sensitive information by the courts. Rather than simply compelling disclosure of privileged information for open court review, it may be appropriate for the executive branch to satisfy the court in secret chambers of the necessity of nondisclosure." (internal citation omitted))

[52] See Meredith Fuchs & G. Gregg Webb, Greasing the Wheels of Justice: Independent Experts in National Security Cases, Am. Bar Ass'n Nat'l Security L. Rep., Nov. 2006, at 1, 3–5.

[53] Meredith Fuchs, Judging Secrets: The Role Courts Should Play in Preventing Unnecessary Secrecy, 58 Admin. L. Rev. 131, 174 (2006) (describing Judge Louis Oberdorfer's use of a special master to review classified records in camera in Wash. Post v. Dep't of Def., 766 F. Supp. 1 (D.D.C. 1991)); see also Ellsberg v. Mitchell, 709 F.2d 51, 64 (D.C. Cir. 1983) (encouraging "procedural innovation" in addressing state secrets issues); Al-Haramain Islamic Found. v. Bush, 451 F. Supp. 2d 1215, 1233 (D. Ore. 2006) (suggesting the appointment of a national security expert as a special master to assist in assessing the effects of disclosure); Robert P. Deyling, Judicial Deference and De Novo Review in Litigation over National Security Information Under the Freedom of Information Act, 37 Vill. L. Rev. 67, 105–11 (1992) (exploring the costs and benefits of employing special masters in FOIA national security litigation and concluding that "experience so far suggests that special masters can at least

be employed for limited purposes in such cases, saving court time and facilitating resolution of the issues").

[54] 345 U.S. 1, 7–8 (1953) (internal citation omitted).

[55] Section six of CIPA provides for pre-trial hearings on the admissibility of classified evidence, 18 U.S.C. app. § 6 (2000), during which the court must determine the relevance of the classified information, id. § 6(a), and the adequacy of substitutes offered by the Government in lieu of classified documents, id. § 6(c)

[56] See Vaughn v. Rosen, 484 F.2d 820, 827–28 (D.C. Cir. 1973) (formulating "a system of itemizing and indexing [the allegedly exempt material] that would correlate statements made in the Government's refusal justification with the actual portions of the document" and "would subdivide the document * * * into manageable parts cross-referenced to the relevant portion of the Government's justification"); see also King v. U.S. Dep't of Justice, 830 F.2d 210, 223 (D.C. Cir. 1987) (explaining the "specificity of description" required in a Vaughn index).

[57] Vaughn v. Rosen, 484 F.2d 820, 828 (D.C. Cir. 1973).

[58] Meredith Fuchs, Judging Secrets: The Role Courts Should Play in Preventing Unnecessary Secrecy, 58 Admin. L. Rev. 131, 172 (2006).

[59] See Tenet v. Doe, 544 U.S. 1, 9–10 (2005) (contrasting the "categorical Totten bar" to judicial review of espionage contracts with the "balancing approach" courts must apply in evaluating government claims of "the state secrets evidentiary privilege").

[60] United States v. Reynolds, 345 U.S. 1, 8 (1953).

[61] Id. at 11.

[62] Id. at 9–10.

[63] Zuckerbraun v. Gen. Dynamics Corp., 935 F.2d 544, 546–47 (2d Cir. 1991).

[64] Reynolds, 345 U.S. at 11.

[65] 5 U.S.C. §552(a)(4)(B) (2000).

[66] Id. §552(b)(1).

[67] Reynolds, 345 U.S. at 10.

[68] Thus, with respect to the state secrets privilege, judicial decisions involving the justiciability of espionage contracts, see, e.g., Tenet v. Doe, 544 U.S. 1 (2005); Totten v. United States, 92 U.S. 105 (1875), do not provide relevant precedents. The state secrets privilege neither deprives courts of any grant of jurisdiction, nor does it provide the Government with any grant of immunity.

[69] Reynolds, 345 U.S. at 8.

[70] See, e.g., Am. Bar Ass'n, Report to the House of Delegates 5–7 (Revised Report 116A) (2007); Constitution Project, Reforming the State Secrets Privilege 13 (2007). Judge Patricia M. Wald further testified to the Judiciary Committee that: "our traditions of fair hearing dictate that to the maximum degree feasible all relevant evidence be admitted in judicial proceedings. * * * Only [by inspecting the allegedly privileged materials] can the judge fulfill the judicial obligation to insure [sic] a fair hearing but just as important only if he sees the evidence for himself can he make the CIPA-like decision whether there are alternative ways than its presentation in original form to satisfy the plaintiff's need but not to impugn national security as well as whether the objected to material can be segregated from other material in the same document that does not qualify for protection * * *."—Examining the State Secrets Privilege: Protecting National Security While Preserving Accountability, Hearing before the S. Comm. on the Judiciary, 110th Cong. (Feb. 13, 2008) (prepared statement of Patricia M. Wald).

[71] The segregation of sensitive from non-sensitive information is a feature of FOIA, which requires that "[a]ny reasonably segregable portion of a record shall be provided to any person requesting such record after deletion of the portions which are exempt." 5 U.S.C. § 552(b) (2000). The "reasonable" standard in FOIA's segregation requirement is replaced here with a "possible" standard, in recognition of the unique potency of the state secrets privilege.

[72] Ellsberg v. Mitchell, 709 F.2d 51, 57 (D.C. Cir. 1983); see also id. ("[T]he privilege may not be used to shield any material not strictly necessary to prevent injury to national security ***.")

[73] See, e.g., El-Masri v. United States, 479 F.3d 296, 305 (4th Cir. 2007); Ctr. for Nat'l Sec. Studies v. U.S. Dep't of Justice, 331 F.3d 918, 928–31 (D.C. Cir. 2003); North Jersey Media Group, Inc. v. Ashcroft, 308 F.3d 198, 219 (3d Cir. 2002); Kasza v. Browner, 133 F.3d 1159, 1166 (9th Cir. 1998); Al-Haramain Islamic Foundation, Inc. v. Bush, 451 F. Supp. 2d 1215, 1220 (D. Or. 2006); Edmonds v. U.S. Dept. of Justice, 323 F. Supp. 2d 65, 77–78 (D.D.C. 2004)

[74] Scholars' Letter to Senate Judiciary Committee 1 (Feb. 12, 2008).

[75] See United States v. Nixon, 418 U.S. 683, 708–10 (1974) (stating that "privilege [assertions] must be considered in light of our historic commitment to the rule of law," that "[t]he need to develop all relevant facts in the adversary system is both fundamental and comprehensive," that "[t]he very integrity of the judicial system and public confidence in the system

depend on full disclosure of all the facts, within the framework of the rules of evidence," and that because evidentiary privileges act "in derogation of the search for the truth," they are "not lightly created nor expansively construed"); see also Univ. of Pennsylvania v. EEOC, 493 U.S. 182, 189 (1990) ("Inasmuch as testimonial exclusionary rules and privileges contravene the fundamental principle that the public has a right to every man's evidence, any such privilege must be strictly construed." (internal citations, quotations, and brackets omitted)).

[76] Under FOIA, Congress has authorized Federal courts to determine de novo whether the Government has properly classified information, with the burden of persuasion on the Government. See 5 U.S.C. §552(b)(1)(B) (2000); see also Ray v. Turner, 587 F.2d 1187, 1190–95 (D.C. Cir. 1978) (explaining the legislative history of FOIA and the contemplated role for judicial review, and stating that when Congress overrode President Ford's veto and amended FOIA in 1974 to provide for de novo review and in camera document inspection, Congress "stressed the need for an objective, independent judicial determination, and insisted that judges could be trusted to approach the national security determinations with common sense, and without jeopardy to national security"). In its Committee Report on the 1974 FOIA amendments, Congress indicated that courts in national security cases should "accord substantial weight" to an agency's assertions as to the classified status of the disputed record. S. Rep. No. 93–1200, at 12 (1974) (Conf. Rep.).

Many observers have criticized courts for being too deferential to the Executive Branch in such cases. As one commentator has explained:

"Congress did not direct courts to defer to agency determinations. Instead, it sought to assuage concerns about whether judges could be trusted to perform a de novo review by expressing the expectation that agency affidavits would be given substantial weight. * * * Were agencies to provide detailed, common sense, and credible assertions, then they would be given substantial weight."—Meredith Fuchs, Judging Secrets: The Role Courts Should Play in Preventing Unnecessary Secrecy, 58 Admin. L. Rev. 131, 162 (2006). Whatever Congress's intent with respect to the "substantial weight" standard used in the 1974 FOIA Committee Report, it is the understanding of that term articulated by the court in Ray v. Turner, supra, that accurately captures the intent of Congress in this bill.

It is worth noting that the stakes may be significantly lower in FOIA litigation than in civil cases in which the state secrets privilege is invoked. Under FOIA, any person may request a Government record, and no reason need be given. State secrets cases, by contrast, may implicate core issues of constitutional rights and individual liberties, which makes "utmost deference" or any similar formulation all the more inappropriate in this context.

[77] Cf. Halkin v. Helms, 598 F.2d 1, 13–14 (D.C. Cir. 1978) (Bazelon, J., dissenting from denial of petition for rehearing en banc) (warning that without an independent judicial determination of the propriety of state secrets assertions, "the privilege becomes a shield behind which the government may insulate unlawful behavior from scrutiny and redress by citizens"); Comm. for Nuclear Responsibility v. Seaborg, 463 F.2d 788, 794 (D.C. Cir. 1971) ("[N]o executive official or agency can be given absolute authority to determine what documents in his possession may be considered by the court in its task [of determining applicability of a privilege]. Otherwise the head of an executive department would have the power on his own say so to cover up all evidence of fraud and corruption when a federal court or grand jury was investigating malfeasance in office. * * *"); 4 John Henry Wigmore, A Treatise on the System of Evidence in Trials at Common Law §2376, at 3345 (1905) ("The lawful limits of the privilege are extensible beyond any control, if its applicability is left to the determination of the very official whose interest it is to shield his wrongdoing under the privilege. Both principle and policy demand that the determination of the privilege shall be for the judge."); William G. Weaver & Robert M. Pallitto, State Secrets and Executive Power, 120 Pol. Sci. Q. 85, 90 (2005) ("[I]f the privilege protects the executive and agencies from investigation and judicial power, then the incentive on the part of administrators is to use the privilege to avoid embarrassment, to handicap political enemies, and to prevent * * * investigation of administrative action."); Note, The Military and State Secrets Privilege: Protection for National Security or Immunity for the Executive?, 91 Yale L.J. 570, 578–79 (1982) (discussing "the need for judicial supervision of evidentiary privileges to prevent their use as a shield against liability"); Stuart Taylor Jr., Reforming the State Secrets Privilege, Nat'l J., Apr. 12, 2008, at 16 (noting that the Executive Branch "has shown, time and time again, that it cannot be trusted not to use bogus national security claims to avoid exposure of misconduct or embarrassment").

[78] See supra notes 71 and 76 and accompanying text (discussing judicial review under FOIA). Under FISA, Article III judges must independently review the Government's assertion that electronic surveillance is needed for foreign intelligence purposes, 50 U.S.C. § 1805 (2006), and Federal district courts may review highly sensitive information in camera and ex parte to

determine whether the surveillance was authorized and conducted in accordance with FISA, id. § 1806(f). Under CIPA, Federal courts must determine whether and to what extent classified information may be used at trial. 18 U.S.C. app. (2000).

[79] Examining the State Secrets Privilege: Protecting National Security While Preserving Accountability, Hearing before the S. Comm. on the Judiciary, 110th Cong. (Feb. 13, 2008) (prepared statement of Patricia M. Wald). Judge Wald further noted that "[t]o [her] knowledge, there have been no court 'leaks' of any such information," and that "it is neither unusual or unduly burdensome for federal judges to handle classified information; many do it on a daily basis." Id.

[80] Examining the State Secrets Privilege: Protecting National Security While Preserving Accountability, Hearing before the S. Comm. on the Judiciary, 110th Cong. (Feb. 13, 2008) (prepared statement of William H. Webster)

[81] As noted above, under the Freedom of Information Act courts must require the Government to segregate exempt information (such as properly classified material) from non-exempt information, see supra notes 71 and 76 and accompanying text, and the submission of non-classified substitutes is a central aspect of the Classified Information Procedure Act, which expressly provides courts with discretion to deny Government requests to delete specific data from classified materials or substitute summaries or stipulations of facts. 18 U.S.C. app. §4 (2000). See also Fitzgerald v. Penthouse Int'l Ltd., 776 F.2d 1236, 1238 n.3 (4th Cir. 1985) ("When the state secrets privilege is validly asserted, the result is unfairness to individual litigants—through the loss of important evidence or dismissal of a case—in order to protect a greater public value. Often, through creativity and care, this unfairness can be minimized through the use of procedures which will protect the privilege and yet allow the merits of the controversy to be decided in some form.").

[82] In the Reynolds case, both the district court and the appellate court held against the Government when the Government refused to release the accident report—now widely believed not to contain any state secrets—to the trial judge to be read in chambers. See Louis Fisher, In the Name of National Security: Unchecked Presidential Power and the Reynolds Case 56–57, 79–86 (2006).

[83] 18 U.S.C. app. 3 §6(e)(2)(B) (2000).

[84] Cf. In re United States, 872 F.2d 472, 477 (D.C. Cir. 1989) ("Dismissal of a suit, and the consequent denial of a forum without giving the plaintiff her day in court, * * * is indeed draconian."); Fitzgerald v. Penthouse Int'l Ltd.,

776 F.2d 1236, 1242 (4th Cir. 1985) ("[D]enial of the forum provided under the Constitution for resolution of disputes is a drastic remedy that has rarely been invoked."); Hepting v. AT&T Corp., 439 F. Supp. 2d 974, 995 (N.D. Cal. 2006) (recognizing that "the state secrets privilege has its limits" and that "the court * * * takes seriously its constitutional duty to adjudicate the disputes that come before it").

[85] See In re Sealed Case, 494 F.3d 139, 148–49 (D.C. Cir. 2007) (discussing precedent for the "valid defense" standard, under which if the "court can determine that the defendant will be deprived of a valid defense based on the privileged materials, it may properly dismiss the complaint")

[86] Cf. Examining the State Secrets Privilege: Protecting National Security While Preserving Accountability, Hearing before the S. Comm. on the Judiciary, 110th Cong. (Feb. 13, 2008) (prepared statement of H. Thomas Wells, Jr., President-Elect, American Bar Association) ("To state this more plainly, if the plaintiff could prove the essential elements of his claim without privileged information, the case would be allowed to proceed as long as the government could fairly defend against the claim without having to use privileged information. However, if the government would have its hands tied behind its back by not being able to invoke essential privileged information in defending against the plaintiff's case, the case would be dismissed.").

[87] See, e.g., Kasza v. Browner, 133 F.3d 1159, 1166 (9th Cir. 1998); Al-Haramain Islamic Foundation, Inc. v. Bush, 507 F.3d 1190, 1200 (9th Cir. 2007).

[88] See, e.g., El-Masri v. United States, 479 F.3d 296, 306 (4th Cir. 2007).

[89] See 18 U.S.C. app. §7 (2000)

[90] See 18 U.S.C. app §9 (2000).

[91] Cf. F.T.C. v. Owens-Corning Fiberglas Corp., 626 F.2d 966, 970 (D.C. Cir. 1980) ("Release to a congressional requestor is not a public disclosure * * *. Once documents are in congressional hands, courts must presume that the committees of Congress will exercise their powers responsibly and with due regard for the rights of affected parties." (internal citations and quotations omitted)); Exxon Corp. v. F.T.C., 589 F.2d 582, 589 (D.C. Cir. 1978) ("We have * * * held that release of information to the Congress does not constitute public disclosure * * *. Because such divulgement is not public, it does not in itself impair the value of the * * * secrets involved." (internal citations and quotations omitted)).

[92] See, e.g., Barenblatt v. United States, 360 U.S. 109, 111 (1959) ("The scope of the power of [congressional] inquiry * * * is as penetrating and far-

reaching as the potential power to enact and appropriate under the Constitution."); Watkins v. United States, 354 U.S. 178, 187 (1957) ("The power of the Congress to conduct investigations is inherent in the legislative process."); McGrain v. Daugherty, 273 U.S. 135, 174 (1927) ("[T]he power of inquiry—with process to enforce it—is an essential and appropriate auxiliary to the legislative function. It was so regarded and employed in American legislatures before the Constitution was framed and ratified. Both houses of Congress took this view of it early in their history * * * and both houses have employed the power accordingly up to the present time."); see also Eastland v. U.S. Servicemen's Fund, 421 U.S. 491, 509 (1975) ("Nor is the legitimacy of a congressional inquiry to be defined by what it produces. The very nature of the investigative function—like any research—is that it takes the searchers up some 'blind alleys' and into nonproductive enterprises. To be a valid legislative inquiry, there need be no predictable end result."); Woodrow Wilson, Congressional Government 303 (1913) ("It is the proper duty of a representative body to look diligently into every affair of government and to talk much about what it sees. * * *. Unless Congress have and use every means of acquainting itself with the acts and the disposition of the administrative agents of the government, the country must be helpless to learn how it is being served and unless Congress both scrutinize these things and sift them by every form of discussion, the country must remain in embarrassing, crippling ignorance of the very affairs which it is most important that it should understand and direct. The informing function of Congress should be preferred even to its legislative function. The argument is not only that discussed and interrogated administration is the only pure and efficient administration, but, more than that, that the only really self-governing people is that people which discusses and interrogates its administration.")

[93] 50 U.S.C. § 1806(f) (2000); see also In re Nat'l Sec. Agency Telecommunications Records Litigation, 2008 WL 2673772, at *1 (N.D. Cal. July 2, 2008) (finding that "FISA preempts the state secrets privilege in connection with electronic surveillance for intelligence purposes and would appear to displace the state secrets privilege for purposes of plaintiffs' claims")

Section VII. Minority Views

[1] Black's Law Dictionary 135 (3d ed. 1933).

[2] See William G. Weaver & Danielle Escontrias, Origins of the State Secrets Privilege 17 (2008) (unpublished manuscript) (quoting 12 Co. Rep. 50, 53 (c. 1607)).

[3] William Blackstone, Commentaries on the Laws of England 230–31 (photo. reprint 1992) (1765) ("[A]rcana imperii [state secrets] * * * was not suffered to be pried into by any but such as were initiated in it's [sic] service.").

[4] See United States v. Burr, 25 F. Cas. 30 (C.C.D. Va. 1807) (No. 14692D); see also In re United States, 872 F.2d 472, 474–75 (D.C. Cir. 1989) (tracing the roots of the privilege in this country to United States v. Burr).

[5] Burr, 25 F.Cas. at 37.

[6] 345 U.S. 1 (1953). The Reynolds case has been criticized as being interpreted on an incorrect understanding of the facts. See S. Rep. No. 110–TBA at 3 n.3 (2008) (draft Committee report circulated by Chairman Leahy to accompany S. 2533). The state secrets privilege existed before Reynolds, and has been applied in scores of cases since. In Reynolds, Chief Justice Vinson, who had served in all three branches of government, set out a workable framework for analyzing assertions of the privilege. This framework has since been adopted by every court that has faced these questions. That the Truman administration may or may not have overstated their case one time over a half-century ago does not, in our view, impeach the validity of the court-crafted state secrets doctrine.

[7] See United States v. Nixon, 418 U.S. 683, 710 (1974) ("Nowhere in the Constitution * * * is there any explicit reference to a privilege of [Presidential] confidentiality, yet to the extent this interest relates to the effective discharge of a President's powers, it is constitutionally based.").

[8] Reynolds, 345 U.S. at 10.

[9] See id., at 7.

[10] Id. at 8 ("The court itself must determine whether the circumstances are appropriate for the claim of privilege, and yet do so without forcing a disclosure of the very thing the privilege is designed to protect.")

[11] See, e.g., Nixon 418 U.S. 683.

[12] Reynolds, 345 U.S. at 11.

[13] Id.

[14] Id.

[15] 154 Cong. Rec. S198–02 (2008) (statement of Sen. Kennedy).

[16] See S. Rep. No. 110–TBA at 4 (2008) (draft Committee report circulated by Chairman Leahy to accompany S.2533).

[17] Ellsberg v. Mitchell, 709 F.2d 51, 63–64 (D.C. Cir. 1983); see, e.g., Hepting v. AT&T, 439 F. Supp. 2d 974 (N.D. Cal. 2006) (citing Ellsberg's call for "procedural innovation" in crafting procedures to aid the court in its review of putatively privileged materials).

[18] Ellsberg, 709 F.2d at 63.

[19] Reynolds v. United States, 345 U.S. 1, 11 (1953).

[20] Id. at 9–10.

[21] 439 F. Supp. 2d 974 (N.D. Cal. 2006).

[22] See Reynolds, 345 U.S. at 9–10.

[23] See id. at 11; See also, e.g., Al-Haramain Islamic Found., Inc. v. Bush, 507 F.3d 1190, 1203 (9th Cir. 2007) ("We take very seriously our obligation to review the documents with a very careful, indeed a skeptical, eye, and not to accept at face value the government's claim or justification of privilege."

[24] Reynolds, 345 U.S. at 7–8.

[25] Id.

[26] El-Masri v. United States, 479 F.3d 296, 305 (4th Cir. 2007).

[27] See Al-Haramain, 507 F.3d at 1203–04 ("We are satisfied that the basis for the privilege is exceptionally well documented. Detailed statements underscore that disclosure of information concerning the Sealed Document and the means, sources and methods of intelligence gathering in the context of this case would undermine the government's intelligence capabilities and compromise national security."); El-Masri 479 F.3d at 312 ("[T]he reasons for the United States' claim of the state secrets privilege and its motion to dismiss were explained largely in the Classified Declaration, which sets forth in detail the nature of the information that the Executive seeks to protect and explains why its disclosure would be detrimental to national security.").

[28] S. Rep. No. 110–TBA at 12 (2008) (Majority report circulated by Chairman Leahy to accompany S.2533).

[29] Several academics have accused the Bush Administration of invoking the state secrets privilege more often than its predecessors. However, the only thorough, quantitative study of which we are aware indicates that, while the raw number of assertions of the privilege has increased in recent years, the Bush Administration has not substantively expanded the types of cases in which the privilege is asserted. See Robert M. Chesney, State Secrets and the Limits of National Security Litigation, 75 Geo. Wash. L. Rev. 1249 (2007)

[30] See, e.g., United States v. Nixon, 418 U.S. 683 (1974); In re United States, 872 F.2d 472 (D.C. Cir. 1989); Kasza v. Browner, 133 F.3d 1159 (9th Cir.

1998); Black v. United States, 62 F.3d 1115 (8th Cir. 1995); El-Masri v. United States, 479 F.3d 296 (4th Cir. 2007); Zuckerbraun v. Gen. Dynamics Corp., 935 F.2d 544 (2d Cir. 1991); McDonnell Douglas Corp. v. United States, 323 F.3d 1006 (Fed. Cir. 2003).

[31] Compare U.S. Const., Art. II with id. at Art. III

[32] Even when holding against the government in national security cases, courts acknowledge the Executive Branch's superior national security expertise. See, e.g., Boumediene et al. v. Bush, 2008 WL 2369628 (U.S.) slip op. (Kennedy, J. at p.68) ("Unlike the President and some designated Members of Congress, neither the members of this Court nor most federal judges begin the day with briefings that may describe new and serious threats to our Nation's security.").

[33] Letter of Michael B. Mukasey to Patrick J. Leahy, March 31, 2008, at 3–4.

[34] Al-Haramain Islamic Found., Inc. v. Bush, 507 F.3d 1190, 1196 (9th Cir. 2007).

[35] State Secrets Protection Act, S. 2533, 110th Cong. § 4051 (2008).

[36] See, e.g., El-Masri v. United States, 479 F.3d 296 (4th Cir. 2007); Al-Haramain, 507 F.3d 1190.

[37] See, e.g., Hepting v. AT&T, 439 F. Supp. 2d 974 (N.D. Cal. 2006)

[38] S. 2533 at §4055(1); see also id. at §4054(e)(1) (establishing that evidence is subject to the state secrets privilege if there is "no possible means" of effectively segregating it from other evidence that contains a state secret).

[39] El-Masri v. Tenet, 437 F. Supp. 2d 530, 538 (E.D. Va. 2006) (quoting Sterling v Tenet, 416 F.3d 338, 347–48 (4th Cir. 2005)

[40] Id. at 538–39.

[41] 92 U.S. 105 (1875) (dismissing a claim for breach of an alleged covert espionage contract).

INDEX

D

E

F

G

H

I

J